VOCABULARY FROM
LATIN AND GREEK ROOTS:
A STUDY OF WORD FAMILIES

By: Elizabeth Osborne

Edited by Paul Moliken
Illustrated by Larry Knox

Prestwick House wishes to extend its gratitude to the many contributors whose assistance, comments, and expertise were essential in completing this book.

Prestwick House

P.O. Box 658 • Clayton, DE 19938
Tel: 1.800.932.4593 • Web site: www.prestwickhouse.com

ISBN 978-1-58049-201-0

INTRODUCTION

Prestwick House developed *Vocabulary from Latin and Greek Roots* in response to numerous requests for a solid etymology-based vocabulary program. Because the aim of the program is to increase retention of new words as well as to expand students' vocabulary, we chose to organize the units by meaning rather than alphabetically. A student who associates a root with an idea will be more likely to correctly assess the definition of that root's English derivative.

Each unit contains four Latin and/or Greek roots; two to four English vocabulary words are provided for each root. Unit 13 of this book (pg. 78), for example, contains four roots having to do with seeing and looking. When a student reaches the first root in this Unit, he or she will see the key letters that signal the presence of the root in an English word: VID, VIS. Beneath the key letters is the root from which the English is derived. Students will notice that there are sometimes two forms of the root, and sometimes one. The inclusion of two forms indicates a Latin verb from which English has taken two different forms. VIDERE, for instance, gives us *evident*, meaning "able to be seen," while VISUM gives us *revise*, meaning "to look at again, to edit." When a root comes from a Latin adjective or noun, only one form will generally be included. Greek roots also appear in only one form.

Beneath the definition of the root, the student will find the word, its pronunciation, part of speech, and English definition. In cases in which an English word has multiple meanings, we have chosen to include only the meaning appropriate to the grade level for which the book is intended. The word *refuse* in this book, then, is a noun meaning "garbage" rather than a verb meaning "to deny, to reject;" in Book III, *pedestrian* means "ordinary" rather than "a traveler on foot." In some instances, students may find it useful to review meanings that do not appear and discuss how they are related to the meaning presented.

If the word has a prefix, or if it is especially difficult to reconcile with its root, the entry will contain an analysis of the parts of the word, followed by a literal definition. *Repulsion* in Book III, Unit Five, is explained as *re*, meaning "back," + *pulsum*; the literal meaning is "a pushing back."

Finally, each entry provides a sentence using the word and introduces pertinent synonyms and/or antonyms. For added visual reinforcement of this understanding, mnemonic cartoons appear in each Unit.

Six different kinds of exercise follow the Unit entries. They include three kinds of practice using words in context, one test of a student's ability to infer information based on a word's meaning, one reading comprehension exercise, and one activity in which a student must deduce the meaning of an unfamiliar word based on knowledge of the word's root. By the end of the exercises in each Unit, students will have had thorough practice using the word in context and will be prepared to make the word part of their working vocabulary.

We hope that you find the *Vocabulary from Latin and Greek Roots* series effective in teaching new words and in fostering student interest in the history of our fascinating language.

Note: A guide to the pronunciation symbols and a list of Latin and Greek prefixes can be found at the beginning of this book.

PREFIXES

A (L.) away from
A(G.) not, no
AB (L.) away from
AD (L.)toward
ALTER (L.) another
AMPHI (G.) around, both
ANA (G.) up
ANTE (L.) before
ANTI (G.) against
CIRCUM (L.) around
CO (L.) with, together
CON (L.) with, together
CONTRA (L.) against
DE (L.) down, down from
DIA (G.) through
DIS (L.) apart, away from
DYS (G.) bad
E (L.) out of
EC (G.) outside
EM (G.) in, within

EN (G.) in, within
EPI (G.) upon
EX (L.) out of, away from *
HYPER (G.) over
IN (L.) in, into, on, against, not
INTRO (L.) inside
OB (L.) against
OMNI (L.) every, all
PER (L.) through
PERI (G.) around
POST (L.) after
PRE(L.) before
RE (L.) back, again *
RETRO (L.) backwards
SUB (L.) beneath
SUPER, SUR (L.) above
SYM (G.) with, together
SYN (G.) with, together
TRANS (L.) across
TELE (G.) distant

*Note: *Con, ex, in* and *re* sometimes serve as *intensifiers*. In such cases, these prefixes simply mean *very*.

PRONUNCIATION GUIDE

a = tr<u>a</u>ck   o = j<u>o</u>b
ā = m<u>a</u>te   ō = wr<u>o</u>te
ä = f<u>a</u>ther   ô = p<u>o</u>rt
â = c<u>a</u>re   ōō = pr<u>oo</u>f

e = p<u>e</u>t   u = p<u>u</u>n
ē = b<u>e</u>   ū = <u>you</u>
                          û = p<u>u</u>rr

i = b<u>i</u>t
ī = b<u>i</u>te   ə = <u>a</u>bout, syst<u>e</u>m, s<u>u</u>pper, circ<u>u</u>s

WORD LIST FOR BOOK II

UNIT 1
agile
agitate
allege
enact
energetic
ergonomic
invigorate
prodigal
reactionary
surgical
vigorous

UNIT 2
composure
exponential
hypothesis
imposition
inconstant
instantaneous
parenthetical
reinstate
repository
synthesize

UNIT 3
anticipate
cohabitation
conceive
condone
deceptive
donor
editorial
exceptional
exhibit
intercept
nontraditional
participant

UNIT 4
castigate
chastened
chastise
deify
deity
monotheism
pantheon
polytheistic
sanctify
sanctions
sanctuary
sanctum

UNIT 5
astronomical
celestial
exhume
humility
inter
nebulous
nimbus
stellar
subterranean
terrestrial

UNIT 6
accelerated
demote
discourse
excursion
fugitive
immovable
mobile
refuge
subterfuge
volatile

UNIT 7
avail
consolidate
corroborate
durable
duration
enduring
forte
fortitude
robust
solidarity
valiant
valor

UNIT 8
enumerate
idiom
idiosyncrasy
innumerable
insular
insulate
nonplussed
plurality
single
singular
surplus

UNIT 9
amnesty
connoisseur
demented
diagnosis
mentality
mnemonic
notorious
prognosis
ration
rational
reconnaissance

UNIT 10
autonomous
impunity
jurisdiction
jurisprudence
litigant
litigation
nemesis
perjure
punitive
subpoena
syndicate

UNIT 11
annals
annual
annuity
chronic
chronology
contemporaneous
contemporary
frequent
infrequent
inveterate
tempo
veteran

UNIT 12
abhor
deter
formidable
horrific
intimidate
intrepid
irreverent
revere
terrorize
timorous
trepidation

UNIT 13

advisable
conspicuous
despicable
evident
inoculate
intuitive
ocular
respective
revise
suspect
tutelage
vista

UNIT 14

admission
detract
differentiate
exaggerated
extol
extract
ingest
omission
reference
submissive
suggestible

UNIT 15

cloister
confines
disclose
finite
indeterminate
interminable
preliminary
refine
seclude
subliminal
terminal

UNIT 16

administer
anarchy
arbiter
arbitrary
arbitrate
archaic
magisterial
magistrate
matriarch
minister

UNIT 17

aspersion
disperse
emergent
founder
fundamental
fusion
immerse
intersperse
refuse
sparse
submerge

UNIT 18

assiduous
desist
dissident
insidious
persistent
preside
residual
sedentary
subsidiary
subsist
supersede

UNIT 19

abundant
antediluvian
arid
cataclysmic
deluge
derivative
dilute
redundant
rivulet
torrent
torrid
unrivaled

UNIT 20

appreciative
censor
censure
commensurate
deign
depreciate
dimension
disdain
immense
indignant

UNIT ONE

ERG, URG
Greek ERGON, "work"

SURGICAL (sûr´ jə kəl) *adj.* Very precise; clear and accurate
G. kheir, "hand," + ergon = *hand-work*
The rifle battalion, made up of the best marksmen in the world, targeted its enemy with *surgical* exactness.

ENERGETIC (en ər jet´ ik) *adj.* Active and lively
G. en, "in" + ergon = *into work*
Whenever the weather was too hot, Ethan was not interested in *energetic* activity and preferred to stay home in air-conditioned comfort.
syn: active   *ant:* lazy

ERGONOMIC (ər gō näm´ ik) *adj.* Intended to decrease discomfort and maximize work
G. ergon + nomic, "science or study of" = *study of work*
The *ergonomic* layout of the cockpit helped the pilots focus on flying and reduced their work-related injuries.

The GNOME rearranged his den to make it more ERGONOMIC.

VIG
Latin VIGERE, "be lively, be energetic"

VIGOROUS (vig´ ər əs) *adj.* Done with power, force or energy
Reggie's *vigorous* exercise routine always made him flushed and sweaty.
syn: robust, spirited   *ant:* lethargic, lazy

INVIGORATE (in vig´ ər āt) *v.* To fill with strength and energy
L. in, "into," + vigere = *to put energy into*
The brisk morning breeze *invigorated* the crowds of people walking to work.

▥ *The English word sur-gery comes from a Greek word meaning "to work by hand." We now associate surgery with advanced machines as well as skilled human hands and think of something surgical as being done with machine-like precision.*

IG, AG, ACT, EG

Latin AGERE, ACTUM "do, drive, act"

PRODIGAL   (pro´ də gəl)   *adj.*   Wasting money or resources
L. pro, "forth," + agere = *drive forth, drive away (money)*
Gerald's *prodigal* tendencies eventually left him penniless and on the streets.
syn: wasteful   *ant*: thrifty

AGITATE   (aj´ ə tāt)   *v.*   1. To publicly demand; petition for
2. To move vigorously or violently; to upset
1.   Though the American colonists *agitated* for more power and independence, King George III was deaf to their demands.
2.   Loud noises *agitate* Angela so much that she cannot endure them.

ENACT   (en akt´)   *v.*   To make legal or official
L. en, "in" + actum = *driven into (law)*
As part of the agreement, the United States agreed to *enact* legislation to prevent further environmental damage from greenhouse gases.
syn: decree   *ant*: repeal

REACTIONARY   (rē ak´ shən ər ē)   *adj.*   Strongly opposed to change; conservative
L. re, "back," + actum = *driving back*
The bank preferred to stick to *reactionary* strategies rather than adapt to new conditions.

AGILE   (aj´ əl)   *adj.*   Able to move quickly and lightly
A less *agile* swimmer would never have been able to make the quick turns that Sarita did.
syn: nimble   *ant*: stiff

ALLEGE   (ə lej´)   *v.*   To put forth as true; claim
L. ad, "toward," + litis, "lawsuit," + agere = *to drive towards a lawsuit*
The reporter *alleges* that at four o'clock this afternoon, a local politician took part in an armed robbery.
syn: assert   *ant*: rebut; deny

Ⅲ *One famous story in the New Testament deals with the prodigal son, a spoiled young man who leaves his father and wastes his inheritance, then returns home and seeks forgiveness. Because of this story, some people have come to believe that prodigal means "wandering from home." Don't make this mistake; remember that the son was prodigal because he threw away all of his money.*

EXERCISES - UNIT ONE

Exercise I. Complete the sentence in a way that shows you understand the meaning of the italicized vocabulary word.

1. When the speaker *alleged* that Police Chief Murphy was involved in the scandal…

2. We tried not to *agitate* our teacher today because…

3. Mrs. Prekash's fifth-grade class was less *energetic* than usual because…

4. The *surgical* precision with which the author writes is a sign that he…

5. Manny finds that an afternoon nap *invigorates* him, allowing him to…

6. It is likely that the mayor, in response to the recent wave of burglaries, will *enact*…

7. Polly felt that Dean's views on education were *reactionary* because…

8. Tom was not as *agile* as he once had been because…

9. Devin warned his daughter that unless she stopped being so *prodigal*, she would…

10. Car manufacturers want to design a more *ergonomic* minivan because…

11. My father polished the coffee table with such a *vigorous* motion that…

Exercise II. Fill in the blank with the best word from the choices below. One word will not be used.

energetic   invigorating   alleged   ergonomic   agitate

1. When he discovered that certain students in his class always received higher grades, Marlon _____ that his teacher was showing favoritism.

2. On nights when the talk-show host was not _____, the viewers responded with little enthusiasm.

3. Rather than _____ my dinner guests, the tea I gave them seemed to sap their remaining strength.

4. When the architect described the "Home of the Future," he emphasized _____ details like the sink that made washing dishes easier and faster.

Fill in the blank with the best word from the choices below. One word will not be used.

>   reactionary   agitated   enacted   vigorous

5.   When Cynthia _____ for a bigger room, her parents warned that she was stretching their patience.

6.   When the new president entered office, she repealed many of the regulations _____ by the old one.

7.   Even a(n) _____ shaking was not enough to wake Allen in the morning.

Fill in the blank with the best word from the choices below. One word will not be used.

>   agile   reactionary   ergonomically   surgically   prodigal

8.   Tammy's _____ statements often made the other members of the debate team frustrated.

9.   The bomber pilot knew that unless his aim was _____ accurate, his whole mission would be ruined.

10.   Because it is naturally _____, the cheetah is able to bend and twist its body in mid-stride.

11.   We could tell that Brandon was back to his old _____ ways when he spent two hundred dollars on wine at dinner.

Exercise III. Choose the set of words that best completes the sentence.

1.   Even though the new classroom was supposed to be far more _____ than the old one, teachers still found it impossible to _____ students and inspire them to work.
      A.   agile; allege
      B.   ergonomic; invigorate
      C.   prodigal; enact
      D.   reactionary; enact

2.   Albert's _____, skilled fingers, nimble from years of piano practice, could also handle a video-game console with _____ precision.
      A.   vigorous; prodigal
      B.   agile; surgical
      C.   energetic; reactionary
      D.   surgical; prodigal

3.   Lisa's _____ efforts to have tougher child-safety laws passed inspired others to _____ for the same reforms.
      A.   vigorous; agitate
      B.   ergonomic; allege
      C.   vigorous; enact
      D.   energetic; invigorate

4.   "Although my opponent _____ that I wish to turn the U.S. government upside down," said the candidate, "you must remember that he is _____ and condemns change in any form."
     A.   enacts; prodigal
     B.   invigorates; ergonomic
     C.   agitates; vigorous
     D.   alleges; reactionary

5.   Mother promised to _____ new rules about spending if her children's _____ ways did not change.
     A.   enact; prodigal
     B.   invigorate; reactionary
     C.   allege; ergonomic
     D.   enact; vigorous

Exercise IV. Complete the sentence by inferring information about the italicized word from its context.

1.   Kyle's constant practice made him so *agile* that the other wrestlers couldn't…

2.   The city council *enacted* a tax on cigarettes, but it didn't…

3.   Even though the money's missing, if you *allege* that I stole it, you…

Exercise V. Fill in the blank with the word from the Unit that best completes the sentence, using the root we supply as a clue. Then, answer the questions that follow the paragraphs.

Experts concur that regular exercise is an essential part of a healthy lifestyle, especially for adults who are middle-aged or older. Exercise not only _____ (VIG) the mind and body, it reduces symptoms of anxiety or depression, and it strengthens bones and muscles. Regular physical exertion may also prevent the development of high blood pressure, colon cancer, or diabetes. Despite the obvious importance of physical fitness, however, a recent United States Surgeon General's Office survey indicates that 25% of American adults incorporate little or no exercise into their lives. Another 60% of adults, while occasionally engaging in physical activity, do not exercise on a regular basis. This indicates that only 15% of American adults exercise at levels that truly benefit their health. Communities all over the country are being encouraged to aid their residents in beginning exercise routines. However, before _____ (ACT) a new fitness regimen, older adults should take some precautionary measures to avoid injuries and health complications.

Sufferers of chronic health problems, such as diabetes, heart disease, or asthma, should always consult a physician before beginning a workout program and follow the advice specific to their conditions. For instance, before and after exercising, diabetics should closely monitor their blood sugar levels to avoid bringing on insulin shock or seizures. Heart disease patients should frequently check their heart rates while working out and should never exercise to the point of chest pain. Asthmatics should always carry an inhaler while exercising, since physical exertion may induce an asthma attack. Additionally, if outdoor allergies are a problem, a protective mask should be worn, or outdoor activity should be avoided altogether. It is important for members of these at-risk populations to note that exercise need not be strenuous to be beneficial.

Any man over the age of 40 or woman over the age of 50, even without a diagnosed chronic health problem, should also consult a physician before engaging in a _____ (VIG) exercise program. However, people in this age group may begin a more moderate program of physical exertion without such concern. Anyone beginning a new type of workout should be careful to avoid strain and overexertion. It is important to wear properly cushioned shoes and be trained on any new piece of equipment one may be using to avoid injury. Keeping these precautions in mind will improve the health of adults who are motivated to incorporate physical fitness into their lives.

1.   Which of the following would be the best title for this passage?
      A.   Health Advice for Diabetics
      B.   Precautions for New Exercisers
      C.   The Surgeon General's Survey on Exercise
      D.   The Benefits of Non-Strenuous Exercise

2.   What is the meaning of the term "outdoor allergy" in the above passage?
      A.   a dislike of going outside
      B.   a problem with substances found inside
      C.   a dislike of running
      D.   a sensitivity to substances found outside

3.   What do you think is the author's attitude toward exercising?
      A.   It is important for a healthy lifestyle.
      B.   It is too dangerous for older adults.
      C.   The health benefits are insignificant.
      D.   It will cure all health problems.

4.   The type of exercise any man over 40 should consult with his doctor about is
      A.   moderate.
      B.   yoga.
      C.   vigorous.
      D.   walking.

5.   What could help someone with indoor allergies?
      A.   a mask
      B.   supervision by a doctor
      C.   moderate exercising
      D.   The article does not say.

Exercise VI. Drawing on your knowledge of roots and words in context, read the following selection and define the *italicized* words. If you cannot figure out the meaning of the words on your own, look them up in a dictionary. Note that *graph* means "writer" or "writing," and *pro* means "before."

       To see if Dale was strong enough to work on construction that involved heavy lifting, the doctor decided to test him using an *ergograph*. He asked if Dale had ever undergone such a test. Dale had not. The physician said, "This is necessary for determining your fitness for the manual labor you'll be doing. If you are *proactive*, you can help prevent injuries before they occur."

UNIT TWO

POS, PON
Latin PONERE, POSITUM, "to place, to put"

COMPOSURE (kəm pōs´ zər) *n.* Control over expression and action
L. com, "together," + positum = *put together*, *staying together*
Scott managed to sing three of the songs without laughing, but he lost his *composure* when he saw the goofy face his friend in the front row made.
syn: poise   *ant:* agitation; worry

EXPONENTIAL (eks pō nen´ shəl) *adj.* Steadily increasing
L. ex, "out of," + ponere = *to place out of*
The *exponential* growth of the deer population in the area made us wonder if most natural predators of deer had been eliminated.

IMPOSITION (im pə zi´ shən) *n.* An unwelcome demand; a burden
L. in, "on, onto" + positum = *putting onto*
Because they liked the subject matter they were studying, most of the students did not consider Saturday classes an *imposition*.
syn: bother

REPOSITORY (rə poz´ ə tôr ē) *n.* A place designated for storage
L. re, "back," + positum = *place where things are put back*
The building that was once the train station is now a *repository* for county records.

STAN, STAT
Latin STARE, STATUS, "to stand, stand something up"

INSTANTANEOUS (in stən tān´ ē əs) *adj.* Happening immediately
L. in, "on," + stare = *standing on*
Current Internet connections are so fast that your knowledge of new information can be almost *instantaneous*.

REINSTATE (rē in stāt´) *v.* To bring back into existence or authority
L. re, "back," + in, "in" + status = *to stand (someone) back in*
Fern's supporters marched down the main street of the city urging the local government to *reinstate* her as mayor.
syn: restore

※ *The verb* expound *(ex, "out of," + ponere) means "to explain" or "to express more fully." A mathematical exponent expresses the power to which something is raised. For example, if we were asked to calculate three to the fourth power, the exponent would be four. We say something is growing or multiplying exponentially when it continues to get bigger over time.*

INCONSTANT   (in kon´ stənt)   *adj.*   Not lasting; not steady
L. in, "not," + con, "very, firmly" + status = *not standing firmly*
Just like the director's *inconstant* mind, the film shifts suddenly from one setting to the next.
syn: fickle   *ant*: steadfast

THES, THET
Greek THESIS, "placing"
THETOS, "having been placed"

SYNTHESIZE   (sin´ thə sīz)   *v.*   To combine; to blend
G. syn, "together," + thesis = *placing together*
Cajun food manages to *synthesize* flavors from many different parts of the world and create something entirely new.
syn: integrate   *ant*: analyze

PARENTHETICAL   (pa rən thət´ i kəl)   *adj.*   Explaining the main idea or topic
G. par, "beside," + en, "in," + thetos = *placed in beside*
Paul added numerous *parenthetical* statements to his complicated instruction manual to make it easier to understand.
syn: incidental   *ant*: relevant

HYPOTHESIS   (hī poth´ ə səs)   *n.*   Idea proposed as true; theory
Hilary's *hypothesis* was that water lilies would grow better when exposed to more direct sunlight.
                          ant: fact

The HIPPOPOTAMUS tested the
HYPOTHESIS that he could fly.

EXERCISES - UNIT TWO

Exercise I. Complete the sentence in a way that shows you understand the meaning of the italicized vocabulary word.

1.   The judges were impressed by the spelling-bee contestant's *composure* when…

2.   The *exponential* growth of the residential area in Hinsburg was a result of…

3.   My extended stay at my sister's house may be an *imposition* on her because…

4.   Room 145 of the school is being used as a *repository* for…

5.   The weightlifting coach told her students that muscle growth would not be *instantaneous*, but rather…

6.   The committee decided to *reinstate* Chairman Dorchester when it learned that…

7.   PJ was an *inconstant* supporter of the political party to which he belonged, so he often…

8.   Based on the plants' amazing growth in the presence of Chemical RK-200, we formed the *hypothesis* that…

9.   The composer's new style *synthesizes* both…

10.   Joey felt that he needed to add some *parenthetical* remarks to his speech because…

Exercise II. Fill in the blank with the best word from the choices below. One word will not be used.

imposition   synthesize   composure   reinstate   repository

1.   Marisa feared her _____ would fail her during an especially tough interview.

2.   After several students came to school in clothing that was unacceptable, Principal Levin decided to _____ the dress code.

3.   If doctors are able to _____ the old and new allergy medicines, the result will be a powerfully effective drug.

4.   Hannah's car became a(n) _____ for all the junk that her neighbors threw out.

Fill in the blank with the best word from the choices below. One word will not be used.

      parenthetical   instantaneous   hypothesis   exponential

5.   The effects of the witch's spell were _____, creating a monster where a man had stood one second before.

6.   The increase in people with the disease was not _____, as the doctors had feared; in fact, the disease had begun to disappear.

7.   The botanist's new _____ about marigolds is intriguing, but will probably be proven false.

Fill in the blank with the best word from the choices below. One word will not be used.

      imposition   instantaneous   inconstant   parenthetical

8.   Darlene's _____ affection led her to break up with Jeff several times.

9.   I considered Marvin's constant borrowing of office supplies a major _____ upon our department.

10.   Many of Ben's observations were _____ sentences rather than direct remarks.

Exercise III. Choose the set of words that best completes the sentence.

1.   Agricultural researchers are currently testing the _____ that the modified fertilizer will cause _____ growth in soybeans.
     A. hypothesis; exponential
     B. imposition; parenthetical
     C. repository; inconstant
     D. imposition; instantaneous

2.   Because Rina had dealt with Carl's _____, unreliable emotions one time too many, she lost her _____ and started screaming at him.
     A. parenthetical; repository
     B. inconstant; composure
     C. instantaneous; hypothesis
     D. exponential; imposition

3.   Be aware that in attempting to _____ the two unstable substances, you may cause a(n) _____ and deadly chemical reaction.
     A. reinstate; inconstant
     B. synthesize; parenthetical
     C. reinstate; exponential
     D. synthesize; instantaneous

4. "If it is no _____ on the honorable members of this House," said the member of Parliament, "I propose that we _____ the speaker who was dismissed last week."
    A. hypothesis; reinstate
    B. repository; synthesize
    C. imposition; reinstate
    D. composure; synthesize

5. In a(n) _____ addition to his previous statement, the speaker explained that the building in question had once been used as a(n) _____ for ammunition.
    A. parenthetical; repository
    B. instantaneous; composure
    C. exponential; hypothesis
    D. exponential; repository

Exercise IV. Complete the sentence by inferring information about the italicized word from its context.

1. Because Barbara is an *inconstant* friend, Pete will most likely...

2. When the report notes that gas prices have increased *exponentially,* the data it includes probably...

3. After the professor explains the complicated *hypothesis*, students will be able to...

Exercise V. Fill in the blank with the word from the Unit that best completes the sentence, using the root we supply as a clue. Then, answer the questions that follow the paragraphs.

Composing popular music is not only an art form, but a gift. Songwriters must tell a very detailed story with a beginning, a middle, and an end, and do it all within just a few minutes. On top of that, they must remember that the music should be appealing to the people who will listen to it. That may mean writing a song about a subject a lot of people understand or creating a song with a great sound. Does writing what the public wants to hear, though, take away from the craftsmanship of songwriting? Should songwriting be a matter of creativity, or should it be a matter of business?

Many songwriters today treat their "art" as a day-to-day job. Just like any other working person, some songwriters get up in the morning, get dressed, and drive to an office. Once in the office, they consider it no _____(POS) to spend eight hours a day working. They might work for years until they can come up with a hit song, but the pressure to write good songs is constant. Although songwriters are paid a little bit of money every time one of their songs is played on the radio, they really cannot expect to make an _____(STAN) fortune from one hit song. Instead, they need to write dozens of great songs to be able to make a living.

However, all this pressure to succeed and write hits is destroying the artistry of songwriting. Because songwriters are always trying to write the next big hit song, they do not write about what they feel. Instead, they write only the songs that they think will sell CD's. They may write songs that have a good beat and catchy words, but the songs lack emotional substance. Many of the songs that are popular today seem synthetic because they lack any feelings. If the public seems to want loud, harsh music, songwriters will write about anger or pain; if calm, easy-sounding songs are popular, songwriters concentrate on writing composed, tranquil lyrics.

When songwriters were first paid for their songs, they wrote about their observations of life or about things that had happened to them or to people they knew. They wrote songs that made people happy or made people cry. They wrote from their hearts. Now, however, because songwriting has become a job like any other, with money as the only reward, there is little room for songwriters to be creative. Instead, they must write whatever they think the public wants. Otherwise, they have no chance to sell their songs. It is because of this need to succeed that songwriting, as a craft, is being lost.

1. After reading this selection, we can assume that the author
    A. thinks that few people like music.
    B. thinks that songs should not be played on the radio.
    C. thinks that the art of writing music is very important.
    D. thinks more people should become songwriters.

2. According to the passage, many songwriters are not rich because
    A. they must write a lot of hit songs to make a lot of money.
    B. it takes years to write a good song.
    C. they are not serious about succeeding.
    D. they are not good businesspeople.

3. What is the main idea of this passage?
    A. Writing songs is hard work.
    B. Being a successful songwriter is easy.
    C. Songwriters are not appreciated.
    D. More songwriters are writing music for money, not for art.

4. In this passage, songwriters are compared to what other kind of workers?
    A. office workers
    B. construction workers
    C. singers
    D. musicians

Exercise VI. Drawing on your knowledge of roots and words in context, read the following selection and define the *italicized* words. If you cannot figure out the meaning of the words on your own, look them up in a dictionary. Note that *ex* means "out" and *anti* means "against, opposite."

Though the majority of the works in the great library were destroyed, some are still *extant*. Of these remaining books and manuscripts, one, in particular, has a past shrouded in mystery. Whoever wrote it chose to remain anonymous, probably because the ideas discussed were the *antithesis* of those held by some very powerful political figures. To have such clashing ideas was cause enough for punishment; to publish them would certainly have meant death.

UNIT THREE

CEPT, CIP, CEIVE
Latin CAPERE, CAPTUM, "to take, seize"

INTERCEPT   (in tər sept´)   *v.*   To catch or block
L. inter, "between," + captum = *take between*
Using sensitive radio equipment, the men at Army Headquarters were able to *intercept* enemy signals broadcast from many miles away.
syn: cut off   *ant:* release

PARTICIPANT   (pär tis´ ə pənt)   *n.*   One who takes part in
L. partis, "part," + capere = *take part*
My great-grandmother told us many stories about the days when she was a *participant* in the movement for women's rights.
                              ant: spectator

CONCEIVE   (kən sēv´)   *v.*   To come up with, imagine
L. con, "strongly" + capere = *to strongly take*
Terry *conceived* of the film as a modern-day version of the classic novel *Don Quixote*.

DECEPTIVE   (də sep´ tiv)   *adj.*   Intending to mislead or trick
L. de, "away," + captum = *take away*
Jimmy talks with a *deceptive* calm that hides his true violent tendencies.
syn: false   *ant:* genuine

EXCEPTIONAL   (ek sep´ shən əl)   *adj.*   Standing out from others
L. ex, "out of," + captum = *take out of*
Keith turned his *exceptional* gift for fixing things into a profitable repair business.
syn: unique   *ant:* ordinary, common

ANTICIPATE   (ân tis´ ə pāt)   *v.*   To expect beforehand
L. anti, "before," + capere = *take before*
Because we *anticipated* a drop in sales during the winter months, we tightened our budget for the month of December.
syn: await

HAB, HIB
Latin HABERE, HABITUM, "to have, hold"
HABITARE, HABITATUM, "to have a home, to dwell"

COHABITATION   (kō hab ə tā´ shən)   *n.*   Living together; coexistence
L. co, "together," + habitare = *dwelling together*
The *cohabitation* of coyotes and sheep ranchers is possible, but it requires some compromises.

III *The v in* conceive *was inserted by speakers of French, for whom* concipere *(an altered form of* concapere*) became* concevoir.

EXHIBIT (ek zib´ it) *v.* To show; to display
L. ex, "out," + habitum = *to hold out*
When the children began to *exhibit* signs of restlessness, their babysitter took them for a walk.
syn: demonstrate   *ant*: conceal

DIT
Latin DARE, DATUM, "to give"

EDITORIAL (ed ə tôr´ ē əl) *adj.* Expressing opinions or bias
L. e, "out of," + datum = *given out, published*
A stern look from my father was enough to silence any *editorial* comments.

NONTRADITIONAL (non trə dish´ ə nəl) *adj.* Going against the accepted
        pattern or style
L. non, "not," + trans, "across," + datum = *not given across (time)*
Bert favored *nontraditional* cooking methods that would have shocked his grand-parents.

DON
Latin DONARE, DONATUM, "to give"
DONUM, "gift"

DONOR (dō´ nər) *n.* One who gives something
The bandleader offered a special thanks to the *donor* of the brand-new drum set.
syn: contributor

CONDONE (kən dōn´) *v.* To support; to give approval to
con, "strongly," + donum = *give*
While Mr. Spencer did not punish his boys for their prank, neither did he *condone* their behavior.
syn: allow   *ant*: restrict

*The judge would not CONDONE
what the CON DID.*

EXERCISES - UNIT THREE

Exercise I. Complete the sentence in a way that shows you understand the meaning of the italicized vocabulary word.

1.   Because Yusef was the one who had *conceived* of the robot, he…

2.   As a *participant* in her school's graduation ceremony, Kara was expected to…

3.   Police set up a sting operation in order to *intercept* the stolen money before it…

4.   We quickly learned how *deceptive* a clear blue sky could be when…

5.   A race car driver must learn to *anticipate* the moves of the other drivers so that…

6.   Because he was an *exceptional* athlete, George was often mentioned by…

7.   The principal worried that the teachers were *condoning* bad behavior when they…

8.   People at risk of catching the deadly flu should call a doctor immediately if they *exhibit*…

9.   Because the research paper was full of *editorial* remarks, it seemed…

10. Ginny and Maurice decided on *nontraditional* attire for the dance because…

11. Everyone was surprised by the successful *cohabitation* of…

12. Samantha hoped to find the *donor* of the van so she could…

Exercise II. Fill in the blank with the best word from the choices below. One word will not be used.

donors   deceptive   intercept   condone   editorials

1.   Juan could not _____ the pass because the ball flew over his head.

2.   The radio station must seek _____ who will agree to provide the majority of its funding.

3.   Many vegetarians do not _____ eating meat for moral reasons, but some just dislike the taste of it.

4.   We were worried that the peacefulness of the beach was _____; would we soon be overrun by screaming children, roaring cars, and barking dogs?

Fill in the blank with the best word from the choices below. One word will not be used.

exceptional   anticipate   exhibit   conceive   editorial

5.   Though Wash could play guitar, piano, and trumpet by the time he was seven,
     he did not consider himself _____.

6.   The speech given at our commencement seemed to have a(n) _____ tone rather than a neutral,
     factual one.

7.   Dan was unable to _____ of a world in which there was no hatred or disease.

8.   The jeweler has chosen not to _____ the rare diamond in his store window because he fears it
     will be stolen.

Fill in the blank with the best word from the choices below. One word will not be used.

nontraditional   exhibits   cohabitation   participants   anticipate

9.   Because Cal did not _____ rain, he did not bring an umbrella to school.

10. Though my brother and his fiancée wish to have a(n) _____ wedding, my mother thinks it
     should be organized according to time-honored rules.

11. The tiny room was not designed for the _____ of several people and their pets.

12. Many of the top students in the school were invited to be _____ in a statewide Quiz Bowl com-
     petition.

Exercise III. Choose the set of words that best completes the sentence.

1.   If Marcia does not _____ her friends' cruelty towards Roger, why was she a(n) _____ in
     the round of teasing the other day?
     A.   exhibit; donor
     B.   anticipate; cohabitation
     C.   conceive; donor
     D.   condone; participant

2.   The website explained that applicants for research positions should _____ not only great
     enthusiasm, but also _____ knowledge of the field.
     A.   conceive; editorial
     B.   exhibit; exceptional
     C.   condone; anticipate
     D.   anticipate; deceptive

3.   The director _____ of his new play as having a(n) _____ view on marriage, rather than a strictly conventional one.
     A.   exhibits; exceptional
     B.   condones; deceptive
     C.   anticipates; editorial
     D.   conceives; nontraditional

4.   The seemingly peaceful _____ of the Ferengi Wolf and the Speckled Antelope was _____; they were actually predator and prey.
     A.   donor; exceptional
     B.   cohabitation; deceptive
     C.   participant; exceptional
     D.   donor; deceptive

5.   Unless we can find a(n) _____ who will give us space to show the paintings, we _____ postponing the festival until next fall.
     A.   participant; exhibit
     B.   donor; anticipate
     C.   cohabitation; conceive
     D.   cohabitation; intercept

Exercise IV. Complete the sentence by inferring information about the italicized word from its context.

1.   When Mr. Andersen *exhibits* his enormous strength, other people may…

2.   If you become an organ *donor,* your heart might…

3.   If the author of the monthly newsletter tries to steer clear of *editorial* writing, it may be because…

**Exercise V. Fill in the blank with the word from the Unit that best completes the sentence, using the root
     we supply as a clue. Then, answer the questions that follow the paragraphs.**

The powers of the executive branch of our government now allow a president to act in the best interests of our nation without a formal declaration of war from Congress. When he became president in 1963, Lyndon Johnson didn't have authority from Congress to do the things that he wanted done in Vietnam. He wanted very much to find an honorable resolution to the conflict, but he did not _____(CIP) the strength and determination of the rebels who were fighting for North Vietnam. One day in 1964, an American ship was fired upon while it was in a body of water called the Gulf of Tonkin, which is in what was then North Vietnam. This attack propelled Congress to enact the "Gulf of Tonkin Resolution," which gave President Johnson the authority he needed to increase U.S. involvement in the conflict.

Part of his plan was to raise the number of combat aircraft involved in the fight. The American Air Force con-trolled the skies over Southeast Asia, and pilots seldom had to worry about other pilots defeating them. However, other threats came from land-based anti-aircraft weapons, including the dreaded surface-to-air missiles called SAMs. These missiles were about as large as a telephone pole; they flew at supersonic speed, had radar-guided systems, and were very accurate and lethal. A pilot knew he was under attack when his on-board detection systems warned that a missile was homing in on his aircraft. To survive, a pilot had to "take it down," meaning dive directly for the ground. This drastic maneuver, if successful, would prevent the missile from _____(CEPT) and destroying his aircraft since the missile could not twist and turn as fast as the airplane could. It is hard to _____ (CEIVE) how terrifying a SAM attack could be for a pilot, who had to _____ (HIB) the finest flying abilities under extreme stress, if he did not want to die or be captured.

Despite heavy U.S. presence in Vietnam and control of Vietnamese airspace, President Johnson could not win the war. In the end, it was President Richard Nixon who managed to bring about a peace treaty in 1973. Now, there is one Vietnam, and we no longer refer to the country as divided into North, South, and Central sections. The Vietnam Memorial in Washington commemorates the sacrifice of over 50,000 men and women who died during this undeclared war.

1. What can you infer from the article is the last thing that a U.S. president in the 21st century needs before he or she may send troops to fight overseas?
    A. a declaration of war by Congress
    B. approval of the legislative branch for a specific amount of time
    C. The president can do it if he/she wants and needs nothing else.
    D. the backing of an ally

2. What, according to the passage, finally brought the war to an end?
    A. control of Vietnamese airspace
    B. the presence of 500,000 troops
    C. the 1973 treaty
    D. the Gulf of Tonkin resolution

3. According to the article, why were SAMs so dangerous?
    A. They were as big as telephone poles.
    B. They flew at supersonic speeds.
    C. They were not very accurate.
    D. Both A and B

4. One of the major changes after peace was achieved in 1973 was that
    A. President Nixon was happy.
    B. Vietnam was no longer divided into sections.
    C. the Vietnam Memorial was built.
    D. None of the above

Exercise VI. Drawing on your knowledge of roots and words in context, read the following selection and define the *italicized* words. If you cannot figure out the meaning of the words on your own, look them up in a dictionary. Note that *re* means "again" and *in* means "in."

While Tina was *receptive* to many of the suggestions made by her editor at the magazine, she absolutely refused to listen when he suggested putting advertisements into her articles. "Such a step," she told him, "would not only go against all of my beliefs as a journalist, a citizen, and a representative of the people who read my articles, but would also *inhibit* my style a great deal. My writing would be strained and unnatural if I had to stop every few paragraphs to support some company or product."

UNIT FOUR

SANCT
Latin SANCTUS, "holy"

SANCTUM   (sānk´ təm)   *n*.   A private place; a retreat
To be invited into the holy man's *sanctum* was considered the highest honor among his disciples.

SANCTIFY   (sānk´ tə fī)   *v*.   To make holy
The fifth of every month was *sanctified* as a day of remembrance and meditation.
syn: bless

SANCTIONS   (sānk´ shəns)   *n*.   Something that forces obedience with a law or rule
The National Association of Methodist Priests imposed *sanctions* upon Duttonville United Church when the pastor refused to follow official policy.

SANCTUARY (sānk´ tchōō ə rē)   *n*.   A place of protection
Because hunting was prohibited on the five-mile stretch of land, the forest became a *sanctuary* for all kinds of threatened wildlife.
syn: refuge

DEI
Latin DEUS, "god"

DEITY   (dē´ ə tē)   n.   A god; a divine being
The priests warned that using the name of the *deity* lightly might bring disaster on the community.

DEIFY   (dē´ ə fī)   v.   To make into a god; to treat like a god
History has shown that while we should not condemn the President, neither should we *deify* him.

ant: abase

THE
Greek THEOS, "god"

PANTHEON   (pân´ thē on)   *n.*   A group of gods; a group of people so
        accomplished in a skill or field that they seem like gods
G. pan, "all," + theos = *all gods*
The new book on dance has an extensive section about the whole *pantheon* of
French ballet greats.

POLYTHEISTIC   (po lē thē is´ tək)   *adj.*   Having several gods or deities
G. poly, "many," + theos = *many gods*
Some of the greatest artworks of the fundamentally *polytheistic* culture show the
various gods feasting together.

MONOTHEISM   (mo nō thē´ izm)   *n.*   Worship of or belief in only one god
G. monos, "one," + theos, "gods," = *one god*
Judaism, Islam, and Christianity are all based upon *monotheism* because they have
a single, all-powerful deity at their centers.

CAST, CHAST
Latin CASTUS, "pure"

CASTIGATE   (kas´ tə gāt)   *v.*   To criticize; to condemn
Sports fans around the world *castigated* the batter for his involvement in the
scandal.

CHASTENED   (chā´ sənd)   *adj.*   Made less proud; humbled
Chastened by the failure of the plan she had spent months developing, Kathy took
some time off to rethink her strategy.

CHASTISE   (chas´ tīz)   *v.*   To punish verbally; to scold
No matter how many times I *chastised* Dominic for leaving his shoes in the
kitchen, he could not seem to break the habit.

▣ *The Latin* castus, *from
which we get the word*
chaste, *meaning "pure,"
has given us several
English words relating
to scolding or punish-
ment. Why do you think
this is the case?*

▣ *A caste system divides
people into levels based
on their supposed purity
or value. Your snobby
neighbors, for instance,
might consider their
peers to be in a lower
caste.*

EXERCISES - UNIT FOUR

Exercise I. Complete the sentence in a way that shows you understand the meaning of the italicized vocabulary word.

1.   New churchgoers could only be *sanctified* by…

2.   Walter was *castigated* by the other members of the wrestling team for…

3.   The attic was Holly's *sanctum*, and she often went there when…

4.   In order to provide a *sanctuary* for the people fleeing the war, immigration officials…

5.   The *polytheistic* tendencies of the ancient Greeks are evident in their…

6.   The president promised to lift *sanctions* against the opposing nation only if…

7.   Journalists seemed almost ready to *deify* the candidate they thought had…

8.   The book examines the *pantheon* of great American athletes, paying special attention to…

9.   Esther is a strong believer in *monotheism* because…

10.   Millicent returned from her summer vacation *chastened* by…

11.   Kevin *chastised* his younger siblings for…

12.   Villagers often performed good works in the hopes that the *deity* would…

Exercise II. Fill in the blank with the best word from the choices below. One word will not be used.

        castigate   polytheistic   sanctified   sanctum   chastened

1.   The criminal mastermind's preferred _____ was a dark room at the back of a restaurant.

2.   As she grew up, Tia moved from a belief in one all-powerful creator to a more _____ system.

3.   "This battleground," said the speaker, "has been _____ by the blood of those who fought and died here."

4.   Dennis was so _____ by his teacher's disapproval that he rewrote his entire paper.

Fill in the blank with the best word from the choices below. One word will not be used.

> deity   sanctuary   sanction   pantheon   deified

5. Zeus was a(n) _____ who had absolute power over the universe and all mankind.

6. The general's victory on that day _____ him in the eyes of his troops, who watched in awe as he rode by.

7. The entire _____ of great contemporary artists was represented in the new exhibit.

8. The library was a(n) _____ for those children who would not or could not participate in the games outside.

Fill in the blank with the best word from the choices below. One word will not be used.

> monotheism   castigates   sanctifies   chastising   sanctions

9. Father Torrance said that _____ requires that the divine being have total control.

10. The latest editorial _____ the school board for placing too much emphasis on passing tests.

11. Heavy _____ on trade made it impossible to buy many things that had once been readily available.

12. Rather than _____ me for being late, my father said he was glad I was safe.

Exercise III. Choose the set of words that best completes the sentence.

1. _____ by his loss to an inferior chess player, Rick shut himself in the _____ of his room and began going over the game he had lost.
   A. Chastened; sanctum
   B. Deified; sanctuary
   C. Polytheistic; sanctum
   D. Castigated; monotheism

2. It makes no sense to _____ the doctor for coming up with the surgical procedure and yet _____ his students for actually using it on patients.
   A. sanctify; deify
   B. castigate; chastise
   C. deify; castigate
   D. sanctify; chastise

3. In searching for ways to punish the rebellious colony, the legislature discussed many forms of _____; in the end, however, the colony's leaders were mildly _____ and allowed to go on their way.
   A. deity; sanctified
   B. sanction; deified
   C. monotheism; chastened
   D. sanction; chastised

4.   Would the young basketball player be remembered as a _____ in the _____ of sports greats, or would he disappoint his fans and be forgotten?
       A.   sanctuary; deity
       B.   sanction; monotheism
       C.   deity; pantheon
       D.   sanctum; pantheon

5.   The new government promised to provide _____ for converts to the new religion, who were being harassed for their _____ beliefs.
       A.   sanctum; chastened
       B.   sanctuary; polytheistic
       C.   deity; pantheon
       D.   monotheism; sanctified

Exercise IV. Complete the sentence by inferring information about the italicized word from its context.

1. If Mrs. Miller *castigates* her neighbor for his parties, he may…

2. The ancient Egyptians *deified* their kings after death, indicating that they believed…

3. If Liz tells you she memorized the *pantheon* of gods and goddesses before the big mythology test, you can probably assume she knows…

Exercise V. Fill in the blank with the word from the Unit that best completes the sentence, using the root we supply as a clue. Then, answer the questions that follow the paragraphs.

The killing of whales for food began off the coasts of many different countries approximately 3,000 years ago. Female whales would come close to shore in order to give birth; the shallow waters, abundant food for the mothers, and protected coastlines provided a _____ (SANCT) for their "calves," as whale babies are called, until the newborns were able to feed in the open oceans. Because the whales congregated close to shore, primitive hunters did not need large ships or great sailing techniques to harvest what they needed. In addition, these early sailors killed only a few whales each year. Except in the Arctic, there was no way to keep the whale meat, called "blubber," fresh. It had to be used quickly, and, therefore, the population of these huge creatures did not suffer greatly.

During the nineteenth and early twentieth century, however, new uses for the oil found in certain whales led to a dramatic increase in the price of the oil and the deaths of whales. People used oil in lamps to light streets, as an additive in soaps, and, mainly, to lubricate the machines that were invented during the Industrial Revolution. Larger boats that could sail throughout the world's oceans for up to a year at a time made whaling much more efficient. As an example, in 1910, over twelve thousand whales were killed. With improvements in techniques, though, more than forty-three thousand were killed in 1930. Within a few decades, nearly all whale species were close to extinction. Fortunately, whale oil began to be replaced by synthetic materials, and with the passing of new world-wide _____ (SANCT) against commercial whaling, the number of these magnificent mammals is increasing every year.

1.   According to the passage, what is a reason primitive hunters did not kill more whales?
     A.   Their boats were too small.
     B.   They couldn't preserve the meat.
     C.   Sailing techniques were not advanced.
     D.   There was no need for whale oil.

2.   Which is *not* a use for whale oil?
     A.   food
     B.   lighting
     C.   soap
     D.   lubrication

3.   What can you infer is the reason the phrase "Except in the Arctic" is used?
     A.   The Arctic weather could preserve the meat longer.
     B.   The Arctic does not have a protected, safe coastline.
     C.   Whale meat was more necessary in the Arctic than elsewhere.
     D.   More whales swam in the Arctic Ocean, making hunting easier.

Exercise VI. Drawing on your knowledge of roots and words in context, read the following selection and define the *italicized* words. If you cannot figure out the meaning of the words on your own, look them up in a dictionary. Note that *sacro* means "holy" and *apo* means "change into."

The name of the football legend is still *sacrosanct* in the halls of the University. People whisper in awe of the day he ran eighty yards to score a winning touchdown in the last minute of a game that was played from start to finish in heavy snow. It seemed, at the moment of his victory, that he underwent a kind of *apotheosis* in the eyes of his fans: for the rest of his life, he would be approached by supporters who saw him as divine, or at least divinely inspired.

UNIT FIVE

HUM
Latin HUMUS, "ground, earth"

HUMILITY (hū mil´ ə tē) *n.* Lack of pride; modesty
Although the leader had influenced the lives of thousands of people, he always spoke with the utmost *humility*.

EXHUME (ək zōōm´) *v.* To remove from the ground; dig up
L. ex, "out of," + humus = *out of the ground*
In order to prove his theory about the murder, the District Attorney ordered that the body be *exhumed*.

ant: bury

The detective ZOOMED to EXHUME the body.

> ▥ *The English words* hum-ble *and* humility *both come from humus. To be* humble, *or to show* humility, *you must be close to the ground rather than proudly raising yourself above others.*

STELL
Latin STELLA, "star"

STELLAR (stəl´ ər) *adj.* Excellent; outstanding
For her *stellar* performance in her first year at the company, Emily was honored with a special luncheon.

ant: subpar

ASTR
Greek ASTRON, "star"

ASTRONOMICAL (as trə nom´ ə kəl) *adj.* Enormous; immense
The *astronomical* cost of gasoline forced many citizens to start taking the bus.
syn: huge   *ant*: tiny

> ▥ Astronomy *is literally the "study of stars," a field of learning which covers outer space and objects in outer space. Something* astronomical *can relate to this study or can be as huge as the stars are high.*

NEB, NIMB

Latin NEBULA, "cloud"
NIMBUS, "cloud"

NEBULOUS (neb´ yōō ləs) *adj.* Not definite; vague
When the student gave a *nebulous* answer to the question, his teacher asked him for more information.
syn: uncertain *ant*: clear; understandable

NIMBUS (nim´ bəs) *n.* A cloud
The *nimbus* of fog around the crest of the mountain lingered until a wind came up and blew it away.

CELES

Latin CAELUM, "sky"

CELESTIAL (se les´ shəl) *adj.* Having to do with the sky or heavens
As a child, Inez was always on the lookout for angels and other *celestial* beings.

TERR

Latin TERRA, "earth, ground"

TERRESTRIAL (te res´ trē əl) *adj.* Earthly; of or from land
Studies of the mysterious creature have failed to determine whether it is mainly *terrestrial* or not.
ant: extraterrestrial

INTER (in ter´) *v.* To put into the ground; to bury
L. in, "in," + terra = *in the ground*
The solemn ceremony ended when the body had been *interred,* and the priest had given the blessing.

SUBTERRANEAN (sub ter ā´ nē ən) *adj.* Beneath the ground
L. sub, "beneath," + terra = *under the earth*
Because the money was hidden deep in a *subterranean* cavern, it was not discovered for many years.
ant: aboveground

▥ *A nebula is a cloud of gas and dust in outer space; its shape constantly changes.*

EXERCISES - UNIT FIVE

Exercise I. Complete the sentence in a way that shows you understand the meaning of the italicized vocabulary word.

1.   Even animals with *subterranean* habits must occasionally…

2.   The ancient Greek gods were said to have a *celestial* home rather than…

3.   I have always thought that Morton was a *stellar* actor because he…

4.   Nick admitted his mistake with such *humility* that we all…

5.   Harmony's ideas about her upcoming English paper were so *nebulous* that we wondered if…

6.   The body of the murder victim had to be *exhumed* so that…

7.   While one species of bird is primarily *terrestrial*, its cousin…

8.   A *nimbus* of smoke hung over the mountain like…

9.   When the citizens tried to *inter* their Nazi past, they found that they could not…

10.   The *astronomical* increase in housing costs led many people to…

Exercise II. Fill in the blank with the best word from the choices below. One word will not be used.

nimbus   subterranean   celestial   stellar   exhume

1.   The journalist wondered whether she should _____ the long-dead controversy simply for the sake of a story.

2.   A(n) _____ of mosquitoes seemed to surround my head every time I went outside.

3.   Anthony's _____ accomplishments as a woodworker are reflected in his numerous awards.

4.   On some _____ transit systems, passengers do not see daylight for up to an hour.

Fill in the blank with the best word from the choices below. One word will not be used.

terrestrial   celestial   nebulous   humility

5.   The _____ splendor of the Northern Lights has amazed stargazers for centuries.

6.   As I read more, my _____ understanding of photosynthesis became clear and sharp.

7.   Though the commentators found the tennis player somewhat lacking in _____, they had to agree with him that he was the best player in history.

Fill in the blank with the best word from the choices below. One word will not be used.

inter   astronomical   terrestrial   stellar

8.   The farmers who found the strange object believed that it was not _____ in origin, but had fallen from the sky.

9.   The children wished to _____ the gerbil that had died.

10.   The cost of vegetables at the neighborhood store is high, but not _____.

Exercise III. Choose the set of words that best completes the sentence.

1.   The _____ that Howard showed when talking about his academic work gave no hint of his _____ performance in school.
    A. humility; stellar
    B. nimbus; astronomical
    C. nebula; subterranean
    D. nimbus; terrestrial

2.   In order to _____ the buried city, archaeologists first had to map a series of _____ water tunnels that wove in and out of the area.
    A. inter; astronomical
    B. exhume; subterranean
    C. exhume; stellar
    D. inter; celestial

3.   When a member of the royalty died, he or she was _____ in a grand tomb, and _____ conditions—alignment of the sun, moon, stars, and planets—were recorded in the book of the priests.
    A. stellar; terrestrial
    B. exhumed; stellar
    C. nimbus; celestial
    D. interred; celestial

4.   Even people who have seen the strange, rare creature can give only _____ descriptions of its size
     and speed; all that we know for sure is that it is _____ in habitat.
     A. astronomical; stellar
     B. celestial; astronomical
     C. nebulous; astronomical
     D. nebulous; terrestrial

5.   On the night when the holy man appeared on television, his head bathed in a(n) _____ of light,
     ratings for the network were _____.
     A. nebula; terrestrial
     B. celestial; stellar
     C. nimbus; astronomical
     D. nebula; subterranean

Exercise IV. Complete the sentence by inferring information about the italicized word from its context.

1.   If Sheila takes a course on *terrestrial* mammals, she should be prepared to study...

2.   The review for the horror movie mentioned *exhuming* bodies, so I think...

3.   Roberto speaks of his accomplishments with such *humility* that it seems...

**Exercise V. Fill in the blank with the word from the Unit that best completes the sentence, using the root
          we supply as a clue. Then, answer the questions that follow the paragraphs.**

During the Age of Exploration, many a mariner became lost at sea, even with the best of charts and compasses. Sailors died when ships swept upon rocks, and the gold and goods of nations were lost. To avoid such _____ (ASTR) disasters, navigators needed to determine their exact whereabouts—their latitude and longitude.

The lines of latitude, which parallel the equator, circle the earth; the lines of longitude do the same, but they run north to south. Both lines together create an imaginary grid, which enables sailors to pinpoint their exact position on the Earth. Latitude can be determined by the length of day, the position of the sun, or the stars in the sky. Longitude, however, is a much more complicated matter, because it is partly determined by time. One needs to know what time it is aboard ship and what time it is at a place of known longitude, at the very same moment. The difference in time can then be translated into a geographical separation by a simple calculation. The earth takes twenty-four hours to complete a revolution (three hundred sixty degrees). Therefore, one hour equals one twenty-fourth of a spin, or fifteen degrees.

What, one might ask, was the problem? Couldn't the ship's captain check the time when he left the port, then check his clock out at sea? That would be easy today, in the era of cheap wristwatches. However, the older ocean explorations took place in the era of pendulum clocks. On a rolling ship, such clocks would slow down, speed up, or stop altogether; changes in temperature would also thin or thicken a clock's lubricating oil, which interfered with proper running. Other factors affecting such clocks were barometric pressure or variations in the earth's gravity from one latitude to another. There was absolutely no way to tell exact time, so sailors had to guess or estimate their location. The great astronomers and scientists of the day struggled with one method after another, hoping to find a solution to the problem. Governments of the great maritime nations, including England, Spain, the Netherlands, and Italy, offered huge rewards to anyone discovering how to determine longitude. England's prize was the largest: the equivalent of several million dollars in today's currency.

It was an English clockmaker, John Harrison, a man of humble birth but high intelligence, who solved the problem. He devoted his life to the quest for an accurate way to determine longitude and finally invented a clock that would keep time faithfully from its home port to its destination. His experiments included doing away with the pendulum and using rust-resistant materials (brass and steel) and parts that did not require lubrication.

Many astronomers were jealous of Harrison's success and felt they could find a better answer in _____ (CELES) bodies, but in the end, only Harrison's clock worked. In 1773, aged and tired after forty years of work, Harrison was awarded his prize by King George III.

1. Latitude can be determined by
    A. length of the day.
    B. location of the sun.
    C. position of the stars in the sky.
    D. All of the above.

2. Longitude can be determined by
    A. knowing the exact latitude.
    B. knowing what percentage of 360 degrees one has traveled.
    C. knowing the time at the place of departure as well as the time aboard ship.
    D. All of the above.

3. The best title for this essay would be
    A. Astronomy: Resolving the Mystery of Longitude.
    B. Longitude.
    C. Latitude vs. Longitude.
    D. The Race to Discovery.

4. To make a clock that worked at sea, Harrison needed
    A. a pendulum.
    B. good lubrication.
    C. rust-proof parts.
    D. All of the above.

Exercise VI. Drawing on your knowledge of roots and words in context, read the following selection and define the *italicized* words. If you cannot figure out the meaning of the words on your own, look them up in a dictionary. Note that *trans* means "across" and *colous* means "dwelling in."

The *transhumance* of our herd of Guernsey cows always began in the early spring, when the lush grasses on the south hillsides began to sprout at an incredibly fast rate. During the winter, the herd had been pastured in a field north of the farm, where tougher winter grasses grew in moderate amounts. As the thaw of the ground began, *terricolous* creatures like worms and beetles, in the process of tunneling to the surface of the ground, began breaking apart the tough sod from underneath, allowing the soil to absorb oxygen and nourish young plants.

UNIT SIX

CURS, COURSE
Latin CURRERE, CURSUM, "to run"

EXCURSION   (ek skər´ zhən)   *n.*   A brief pleasure outing
L. ex, "out from," + "cursum" = *running out from*
An extra week's vacation would give us time for an *excursion* into the mountains near our home.
syn: trip

DISCOURSE   (dis´ kôrs)   *n.*   Exchange of words; conversation
L. dis, "apart," + cursum = *running apart*
Discourse between the two sides was halted temporarily because of an outbreak of violence in the capitol.

The obstacle COURSE is no place for DISCOURSE.

CELER
Latin CELER, "fast, swift, quick"

ACCELERATED   (ak sel´ ə rā təd)   *adj.*   Made faster
L. ad, intensifier + celer = *speed*
The *accelerated* rise to stardom of a previously unknown actor was due in large part to his financial connections.
syn: quickened

ant: slowed

VOLA
Latin VOLARE, VOLATUM, "to fly"

VOLATILE   (vol´ ə təl)   *adj.*   Changing often; unpredictable
The *volatile* political situation in the city made people so nervous that they were ready to flee to the country at a moment's notice.

ant: unchanging

▥ *A volant animal is one that can fly. Most, but not all, birds are volant.*

MOV
Latin MOVERE, MOTUM, "to move"

IMMOVABLE   (i mōōv´ ə bəl)*adj.*   Impossible to move or change
L. in, "not," + movere = *not able to be moved*
The housekeeper could not figure out how to clean the floor under the *immovable* chest of drawers.

MOBILE   (mō´ bəl)   *adj.*   Moving; able to move
Rita found herself in need of a *mobile* office when she started taking on clients who lived miles or even states away from one another.

DEMOTE   (dē mōt´)   *v.*   To lower in rank or authority
L. de, "down from," + motum = *moved down from*
Because of his failure to properly supervise the camp's children, Frank was *demoted* from Head Counselor to Assistant Counselor.

ant: promote

FUG
Latin FUGARE, FUGATUM, "to flee"

FUGITIVE   (fūj´ ə təv)   *n.*   Someone who is running away or escaping
After the fire in the prison, two men escaped and became *fugitives*.

REFUGE   (ref´ ūj)   *n.*   Protection or safety
L. re, "back," + fugare = *to flee back*
The political activist, wanted dead or alive by the government, sought *refuge* in the home of some of her supporters.
syn: sanctuary

SUBTERFUGE   (sub´ tər fūj)   *n.*   Trick; act of deception
L. subter, "secretly" + fugare = *to flee secretly*
In order to increase slow sales, Simon employed a *subterfuge* that involved claiming success where there had been none.
syn: trickery

Ⅲ Fugitive *often describes something or someone who is being chased; it can also, however, mean "something that goes away quickly" or "something passing." Thus, you can have* fugitive *feelings of remorse for stealing the cookie, but then convince yourself that it was worth it.*

EXERCISES - UNIT SIX

Exercise I. Complete the sentence in a way that shows you understand the meaning of the italicized vocabulary word.

1.   It was clear that the horse would not be *mobile* until...

2.   Connie was *demoted* from her position as vice-captain of the hockey team because...

3.   The picnickers' *excursion* was cut short by...

4.   We noticed an *accelerated* decline in the economy when...

5.   The hikers desperately sought *refuge* when...

6.   Beth was tired of being a *fugitive* because...

7.   Whoever had constructed this *immovable* piece of furniture had clearly wanted to...

8.   The car salesman employed many kinds of *subterfuge* to...

9.   Because Leah was an emotionally *volatile* person, she often...

10. Extended *discourse* between the boss and his employees resulted in...

Exercise II. Fill in the blank with the best word from the choices below. One word will not be used.

accelerated   refuge   discourse   immovable   volatile

1.   Many directors dreaded working with the _____ actor, who was known to explode into violent rages without warning.

2.   My _____ with Ed continued even after he moved across the country.

3.   Violent weather patterns moving across the Midwest were _____ by a storm system already in place.

4.   We were amazed when the seemingly _____ tree stump turned out to be as light as an empty box.

Fill in the blank with the best word from the choices below. One word will not be used.

excursion demote fugitive refuge

5. Before becoming a(n) _____, Richard had to dye his hair and shave his beard.

6. Although the chef was constantly threatening to _____ David, she was secretly pleased with his work.

7. Tanya went to her grandmother's house seeking _____ from her mother's constant criticism.

Fill in the blank with the best word from the choices below. One word will not be used.

mobile subterfuge excursion accelerated

8. After a few unsuccessful attempts at _____, Claire told her uncle the truth.

9. It was important for the army to be _____ so that it could reach crucial defense points before the enemy did.

10. A weekly _____ to the bakery was a treat to which we always looked forward.

Exercise III. Choose the set of words that best completes the sentence.

1. The country's _____ economy went through a series of drastic plunges and sudden jumps before beginning a(n) _____ downward slide.
   A. fugitive; immovable
   B. volatile; accelerated
   C. mobile; fugitive
   D. volatile; immovable

2. Because the campsite was completely _____, the campers could pack up and go any time they wanted to take a(n) _____ into one of the surrounding towns.
   A. immovable; subterfuge
   B. volatile; refuge
   C. mobile; excursion
   D. fugitive; discourse

3. Wesley used a form of verbal _____ that made _____ with him either tricky or impossible.
   A. refuge; immovable
   B. excursion; fugitive
   C. mobile; discourse
   D. subterfuge; discourse

4.   The children tried to take _____ in their father's arms, but found him as _____ as their mother in his anger.
    A.   subterfuge; mobile
    B.   refuge; immovable
    C.   excursion; fugitive
    D.   discourse; volatile

5.   When it was discovered that Alex was a _____ from another state, his boss was _____ for hiring him.
    A.   accelerated; mobile
    B.   immovable; volatile
    C.   fugitive; accelerated.
    D.   fugitive; demoted

Exercise IV. Complete the sentence by inferring information about the italicized word from its context.

1. The chemistry teacher said, "Don't heat that *volatile* sample or…"

2. Most criminals, especially non-violent ones, use some sort of *subterfuge* to…

3. If the boss chooses to *demote* his least-capable worker, the other employees should probably…

Exercise V. Fill in the blank with the word from the Unit that best completes the sentence, using the root we supply as a clue. Then, answer the questions that follow the paragraphs.

Americans who live in the Rocky Mountains often complain that inexperienced truckers and Eastern tourists need a lesson in mountain driving before turning the key in the ignition and taking the first _____ (CURS) into higher elevations. Novice drivers should be warned that mountain roads are narrow, often with no shoulders or guardrails, and that routes have plenty of sharp turns.

Inexperienced or inattentive drivers tend to treat mountain roads as they do flat roads, sometimes with disastrous results. Vehicle speed is a crucial factor. Most roads that run up, over, and down a mountain are fast, sharp, winding curves called "switchbacks," with speed limits often no higher than twenty miles per hour. These periodic turns enable the traveler to gradually climb to higher elevations without steep upgrades, lessening the strain on the vehicle's engine. However, this method of road design is often impossible for many trucks and recreational vehicles to navigate properly because of their length, so drivers must always be careful of trucks and RV's riding partially or wholly in the wrong lane.

Interstate highways that run over the mountains are easier to cross because they cut a straighter path. Interstates provide an additional lane for slower moving trucks and RV's to use, but dangers still exist. Going up the mountain road, heavier vehicles will strain to reach the summit, sometimes causing engines to quit; the strain may actually bring on vehicle fires. At most peaks, there is a pullover or rest area so drivers—especially truckers—can stop for a period to let engines cool. On way down the road, however, truckers and RV drivers use the additional lane to roll freely, letting the weight of the vehicle provide momentum. So, the vehicles' speed is _____(CELER) going down.

As a result, most vehicle accidents occur on the downside of a mountain. Inexperienced drivers will come upon a sharp turn too fast and may burn away their brake pads in a desperate effort to slow their speed, discovering too late that they needed to decelerate by putting the car in a lower gear. It's a general rule to take this precaution, called "gearing down," at the summit of the mountain, just before beginning the downward ride.

Losing brakes will happen most often to eighteen-wheelers, simply because a full rig weighs many tons and requires much more brake to slow its momentum. Therefore, on the decline of many mountain highways is what's called a "runaway ramp." It's usually a hundred-yard-long dirt road off the right shoulder of the interstate slanted upward that will stop a brakeless vehicle simply by relying on gravity and gravel, provided a driver can keep control of his or her car or truck long enough to reach it. Happy trails!

1.   What is the primary cause of accidents in the Rocky Mountains, according to the essay?
      A. sharp turns
      B. steep inclines
      C. long upward climbs
      D. inexperienced drivers

2.   What causes engines to catch fire on a mountain's rising lane?
      A. heat buildup in exhaust pipe
      B. no oil in the engine
      C. engine strain
      D. None of the above

3.   Why are switchbacks better than a straight road over the mountain?
      A. Drivers prefer a slower ride.
      B. Drivers like curvy roads.
      C. Switchbacks have an additional lane.
      D. Switchbacks reduce engine strain.

4.   Why are mountain roads more dangerous than flat roads?
      A. plenty of curves
      B. narrowness
      C. no guardrails
      D. All of the above

Exercise VI. Drawing on your knowledge of roots and words in context, read the following selection and define the *italicized* words. If you cannot figure out the meaning of the words on your own, look them up in a dictionary. Note that *con* means "together with."

   Although the Parade of the Lilies is *concurrent* with the Christmas holiday in my country, it has little in common with the Christian festival. Both occur at the same time by sheer accident. Early missionaries landed on the island after being stranded at sea for almost six months. Assuming it was Easter, they decided to simultaneously celebrate the holiday and give thanks by covering the streets of the island with the tropical lilies that grew nearby. This tradition continued even after the calendar had been adjusted. The *fugacious* beauty of the lilies dropping like snow always brings a tear to my eye, though the flowers fade as quickly as the season.

UNIT SEVEN

VAL, VAIL
Latin VALERE, VALITURUS, "to be strong"

VALIANT (val´ yənt) *adj.* Brave; courageous
Although the King of Scotland was a *valiant* warrior, he was no match for the Princess of Portugal.
syn: fearless   *ant*: cowardly

VALOR (val´ ər) *n.* Noble courage
The *valor* with which Arthur faced his difficult illness was just one more example of his strong personality.
syn: heroism   *ant*: cowardice

AVAIL (ə vāl´) *v.* To help; to be of use
L. ad, "towards," + valere = *towards strength*
Niles' great wealth did not *avail* him when it came to avoiding a lengthy prison sentence.
syn: benefit

FORT
Latin FORTIS, "strong"

FORTITUDE (fôrt´ ə tōōd) *n.* Strength of mind; bravery
Valerie strongly objected to Lee's claim that women had less natural *fortitude* than men.

FORTE (fôr´ tā; fôrt) *n.* Strong point; skill
Although Fred had been a math teacher at the school for many years, his real *forte* lay in counseling.
syn: strength   *ant*: weakness

DUR
Latin DURUS, "tough, hard"
DURARE, DURATUM, "to last"

ENDURING (en dōōr´ ing) *adj.* Not diminishing; lasting
The family reunion in July has been an *enduring* tradition for us since my great-grandfather first organized it in 1924.
                                                   ant: fleeting

DURABLE (dōōr´ ə bəl) *adj.* Able to last; strong
Kinsey and Nadia's friendship was so *durable* that it survived major arguments, long-distance moves, and many other major changes.
                                                   ant: obsolete

III *One way to say good-bye to someone in Latin was to say "Vale!" This literally means, "Be strong!"*

III *The forte pronounced "for-tay" is a musical term meaning "loud." Forte meaning "strong point, skill" may be pronounced this way too, but is usually pronounced "fort."*

DURATION   (dōōr ā´ shən)   *n.*   The period of time taken by something
Because his seat had been taken, Rodney was forced to stand for the *duration* of the concert.

ROB
Latin ROBUR, ROBUSTUS, "oak, strength"

CORROBORATE   (kə rob´ ə rāt)   *v.*   To back up; support
L. con, "together," + robur = *to strengthen together*
Jan's own experience with raccoons *corroborated* the story that the ranger was now telling.
syn: confirm   *ant*: contradict

ROBUST   (rō bust´)   *adj.*   Strong and hearty
A minor adjustment in diet helped change the weak, lifeless goldfish into *robust*, thriving creatures.
syn: thriving   *ant*: weak

SOLID
Latin SOLIDARE, SOLIDATUM "to make solid"

CONSOLIDATE   (kən sol´ ə dāt)   *v.*   To gather and combine
L. con, "together," + solidatum = *to bring together firmly*
In an effort to *consolidate* information gathered from several different sources, the sheriff's office developed a new, statewide database.
syn: unite   *ant*: separate

SOLIDARITY   (sol ə dar´ ə tē)   *n.*   Support or sympathy; unity
The human rights organization expressed *solidarity* with those people still in the government prison.
syn: togetherness   *ant*: division

Sometimes, SOLIDARITY is a RARITY.

EXERCISES - UNIT SEVEN

Exercise I. Complete the sentence in a way that shows you understand the meaning of the italicized vocabulary word.

1.   When Chief Pete saw the *valiant* effort the firefighters were making, he told them…

2.   This year's corn crop is far more *robust* than last year's, which looked…

3.   Early railroad workers had to possess great *fortitude*, or they would…

4.   Mandy's call for help in getting down from the tree did not *avail* her because…

5.   Because languages were not Wendy's *forte*, she…

6.   The tale of the giant was an *enduring* myth because…

7.   When Jordan learned that the yearly pay increase would be effective for the *duration* of his career, he decided to…

8.   Lance began to doubt the *valor* of his famous ancestor when he learned that…

9.   The 101st and 104th divisions decided to *consolidate* their military strength in order to…

10.   The travelers were forced to seek more *durable* wheels for their wagon when…

11.   When Louise learned that Steve had *corroborated* her story, she felt…

12.   Those people who had managed to escape the cruel dictator held a parade to show *solidarity* with…

Exercise II. Fill in the blank with the best word from the choices below. One word will not be used.

consolidate   durable   corroborate   avail   valor

1.   Because Blake was rather clumsy and the dishes were not very _____, we often heard sounds of crashing and breaking from the kitchen.

2.   The low-ranking soldier showed such _____ in saving his comrade that he was promoted to sergeant.

3.   We could not _____ ourselves of the use of the library since it was closed that afternoon.

4.   Rather than _____ my father's explanation of the magician's trick, my mother told me an entirely different story.

Fill in the blank with the best word from the choices below. One word will not be used.

duration   forte   robust   solidarity   consolidate

5. William was fond of saying that while running was his _____, swimming was his passion.

6. The _____ Liz expressed for her brother when he was accused of shoplifting showed their close relationship.

7. The radio show host's angry guest swore that for the _____ of the program, he would not say another word.

8. Teresa decided to _____ her different banking accounts in order to have an easier time paying her bills.

Fill in the blank with the best word from the choices below. One word will not be used.

enduring   forte   fortitude   robust   valiant

9. The professor's record of achievements for the college is so _____ that we still honor him today.

10. The linebackers on the football team were chosen not only for their physical _____, but also for their ability to think fast on the field.

11. The baby, who had seemed so weak and fragile at birth, was now a _____, healthy two-year-old.

12. Despite the vet's _____ attempt to save the horse's life, it died of the disease.

Exercise III. Choose the set of words that best completes the sentence.

1. The belief that chocolate causes acne has been a(n) _____ idea, despite the fact that scientific evidence does not _____ the claim.
   A. durable; consolidate
   B. enduring; corroborate
   C. robust; avail
   D. valiant; consolidate

2. The _____ with which Abe protected his family from the bear was not surprising, since he had always had a great deal of mental _____.
   A. valor; duration.
   B. fortitude; solidarity
   C. solidarity; duration
   D. valor; fortitude

3. The prisoners had a great deal of _____ with each other, but they could not _____ them-
    selves of the power their numbers gave them.
    A. duration; avail
    B. fortitude; corroborate
    C. valor; consolidate
    D. solidarity; avail

4. The _____, healthy young man was often mistaken for a star athlete, but his real _____ was
    in jazz piano.
    A. durable; solidarity
    B. valiant; duration
    C. robust; forte
    D. robust; solidarity

5. To build a more _____ and lasting source of economic growth, the company will have to
    _____ its various overseas accounts.
    A. durable; consolidate
    B. valiant; corroborate
    C. robust; avail
    D. durable; corroborate

Exercise IV. Complete the sentence by inferring information about the italicized word from its context.

1. When one witness can *corroborate* another person's story of the accident, the police will most likely…

2. If the team members show great *solidarity*, their fans will probably…

3. Because José made a *valiant* effort to win the race despite his injury, the fans…

Exercise V. Fill in the blank with the word from the Unit that best completes the sentence, using the root
we supply as a clue. Then, answer the questions that follow the paragraphs.

Did you know that there is a women's professional foot-ball league? Did you know that Tiger Woods won fewer than half as many golf tournaments as Annika Sorenstam did in 2002? Did you know that the women's basketball team at the University of Connecticut won 55 consecutive games and set an NCAA record?

If you knew more than one of these facts, you are in a very small minority, because women's sports, for the most part, do not appear on television. When they do, they receive poor ratings and complaints from (mostly male) sports fans who cannot see the same _____(VAL) in the efforts of female athletes that they celebrate in men's sports. This lack of understanding comes more from childhood experiences on the playground than from the differences between men's and women's sports. It is on the elementary school playground that children are first impressed with individual demonstrations of skill. Since

young boys are, as a group, stronger and faster than girls, boys usually win these contests. This difference somehow carries on to adulthood and, to many men, makes women athletes inferior in both _____(FORT) and skill.

Let's consider the case of basketball. Both women and men shoot at a rim that is ten feet off the floor, although the average woman is six inches shorter than the average man. People who say that men's basketball is more enter-taining use the fact that the men's game is faster and that slam-dunks are very rare in the women's game. However, women's basketball has superior passing and teamwork. The American fascination with individual performances, created on childhood playgrounds, forms adults who would rather watch scoring than passing. Marketing only rein-forces this trend, because it focuses on individuals rather than on a group.

This seems to be a mostly American condition, though.

Most Americans see soccer as a long, boring game, but it is the most popular sport in the world, played equally well by both men and women. In other cultures, fans appreciate the complex passing and group coordination that lead to each hard-won goal. This one realization may eventually make the popularity of women athletes as _____ (DUR) as the traditional male stars.

1. Which of the following best summarizes the author's main idea?
    A. Soccer is more popular outside the United States.
    B. Women's success in sports is impressive.
    C. More people should watch women's professional football on television.
    D. Women's sports are not as popular as men's sports, even though they deserve to be.

2. With which of the following would the author most likely agree?
    A. Basketball is not a very popular sport in the United States.
    B. Men's focus on individuality makes the United States a superior country.
    C. Women's basketball involves more teamwork than men's.
    D. Women can dunk a basketball as easily as men.

3. What would make the best title for this essay?
    A. Achievements in Women's Basketball
    B. Tiger Woods vs. Annika Sorenstam: Who is Better?
    C. Comparing College and Professional Sports
    D. America's Obsession with Male Athletes

4. According to the author, when are most values based on competition taught?
    A. During adulthood
    B. Never
    C. During early childhood
    D. During sports practices

Exercise VI. Drawing on your knowledge of roots and words in context, read the following selection and define the *italicized* words. If you cannot figure out the meaning of the words on your own, look them up in a dictionary. Note that *pre* means "before, first."

   The *prevalent* emotion at the trial of G.R. Copes was outrage. This young man had been accused of involvement in a crime he clearly had very little or no part in; he had been waiting for a ride from his brother when a man fleeing police in a high-speed chase came around a corner at upwards of eighty miles an hour. Believing himself to be in danger, G.R. ducked into the door of a nearby building. There, afraid for his life, he watched as the fleeing man's car came to a crashing stop in a ditch. Waving what appeared to be a broken bottle, the man, who (it turned out) had a broken leg, called for medical assistance. G.R, still in shock, found himself unable to move. Later, he was arrested, charged with failing to aid an injured person, and threatened with harsh *durance*. Prison would certainly be the wrong place for someone who did what any of us would have done.

A peninsula (paene, "almost," + insula") is a piece of land that extends into water, but is not completely surrounded by water like an island is.

INSUL
Latin INSULA, "island"

INSULAR (in´ sə lər) *adj.* Limited in knowledge or perspective
Cal's *insular* ideas about politics came from his sheltered upbringing and lack of travel outside his hometown.
syn: restricted   *ant*: broad-minded

INSULATE (in´ sə lāt) *v.* To protect from outside influence
The mayor believed that his status in the community would *insulate* him against the negative attention other politicians had been given.

IDIO
Greek IDIOS, "single, peculiar, personal"

IDIOSYNCRASY (id ē ō sin´ krə sē) *n.* A peculiar quality; a quirk
G. idios + syn, "together," + krasis, "mixture" = *one's personal mixture (of habits)*
The general's only *idiosyncrasy* was his insistence that all his soldiers wear blue uniforms.
syn: habit

IDIOM (id´ ē əm) *n.* Speech or phrase specific to a particular language or
        group of people
Because I was unfamiliar with the *idiom* that my Spanish visitor used, I could not follow the rest of what he said.
syn: dialect

NUM
Latin NUMERARE, NUMERATUM, "to count"

ENUMERATE (ē nōōm´ ər āt) *v.* To list separately; to count off
Latin e, "out," + numeratum = *count out*
Joanna was asked by her doctor to *enumerate* the symptoms that had been bothering her.
syn: tally; itemize

INNUMERABLE (i nōōm´ ər ə bəl) *adj.* So plentiful as to be uncountable
L. in, "not," + numeratum = *not able to be counted*
When viewing the *innumerable* stars that dot the midnight sky, I find it impossible not to wonder how big the universe really is.
syn: countless   *ant*: few

PLUS, PLUR
Latin PLUS, PLURIS, "many"

NONPLUSSED   (non plust´)   *adj.*   Baffled; confused
L. non, "no," + plus, "more" = *no more*
The Vice Principal, looking *nonplussed*, asked why there were no students in any of the classrooms.
syn: dumbfounded   *ant:* clear

SURPLUS   (sûr´ plus)   *n.*   Amount beyond what is necessary
L. super, "over," + plus = *over many*
Zoe was able to get cantaloupe at a good price because the store had a huge *surplus* of melons.
syn: excess   *ant:* shortage

PLURALITY   (plōō ral´ ə tē)   *n.*   Greater part; majority
Noting that a candidate needed a *plurality* of votes to win the election, the announcer prepared to read the results.
                ant: minority

SING
Latin SINGULUS, "single"

SINGLE   (sing´ əl)   *v.*   To isolate; to choose
Donna did not want to be *singled* out by the harsh critic for her performance in the play.
syn: screen

SINGULAR   (sing´ yə lər)   *adj.*   Separated from others; unique
Bo was known around town for his rather *singular* habit of walking to school on his hands.
syn: rare; exceptional   *ant:* usual; ordinary

The SINGER'S SINGULAR voice was like nothing we had ever heard.

III *Someone who is nonplussed is so confused that he or she literally can think of nothing more to say or do.*

EXERCISES - UNIT EIGHT

Exercise I. Complete the sentence in a way that shows you understand the meaning of the italicized vocabulary word.

1. When the sailors saw *innumerable* seabirds on the horizon, they knew that...

2. Gary felt that his gift for acting was not *singular*, but rather...

3. Though she tried to *insulate* her children against rudeness and cruelty, Mrs. Hunter knew that...

4. At first, Earl seemed *nonplussed* by the streamers and balloons, but he soon...

5. The store's vast *surplus* of bananas was brought about by...

6. Many *idiosyncrasies* of the famous actor were revealed when he...

7. Doris searched for the perfect *idiom* to...

8. Because a *plurality* of citizens voted to reduce noise pollution...

9. When Don *enumerated* the many difficulties we would face in the mountains, we...

10. Every day, the school nurse would *single* out a child who had...

11. Laura found the little college town a rather *insular* environment because...

Exercise II. Fill in the blank with the best word from the choices below. One word will not be used.

insular   innumerable   idiom   single

1. When Joyce used a(n) _____ unfamiliar to her listeners, she was forced to stop and explain.

2. Our manager did not _____ just one of us out for criticism; he expressed displeasure with the whole department.

3. Due to his rather _____ upbringing, John had tasted few foods besides those cooked by his family.

Fill in the blank with the best word from the choices below. One word will not be used.

idiosyncrasy   surplus   insulate   innumerable   singular

4. Jeremy often tried to _____ his nervous coworker from the chaos raging in the office.

5. One _____ of Rebecca's was her tendency to nap standing up.

6. Ana's _____ knack for remembering phone numbers led the rest of us to seek her help many times.

7. Though _____ spectators used to crowd Times Square on New Year's Eve, this year it was unusually empty.

Fill in the blank with the best word from the choices below. One word will not be used.

surplus   plurality   nonplussed   enumerated   singular

8. A(n) _____ of wheat on the international market was the result of an excellent growing season.

9. Mr. Hooper was amazed when a(n) _____ of his students chose to skip recess for a science presentation.

10. My teacher _____ at least ten reasons why she refused to pass me for the year.

11. Olivia confessed that she was _____ by my sudden change of mood.

Exercise III. Choose the set of words that best completes the sentence.

1. Members of the small, _____ community were _____ when they discovered that a huge city would soon be built on the borders of their town.
    A. innumerable; insular
    B. singular; innumerable
    C. insular; nonplussed
    D. innumerable; nonplussed

2. While some consider Fred's ability to calculate huge sums in his head a(n) _____ talent, others think that it is an irritating _____.
    A. singular; idiosyncrasy
    B. innumerable; surplus
    C. insular; idiom
    D. nonplussed; plurality

3. The employee did not _____ out anyone as the main cause of his resignation, but he did _____ reasons why he found the workplace unpleasant.
    A. insulate; single
    B. single; enumerate
    C. enumerate; insulate
    D. single; insulate

4.   A(n) _____ of fruit in the storehouse on Monday can mean _____ flies and other pests
      on Tuesday.
      A. idiosyncrasy; insular
      B. idiom; singular
      C. plurality; nonplussed
      D. surplus; innumerable

5.   Even if a(n) _____ of parents were very careful about what their children watch on television, it is
      unlikely that the kids would be _____ from all of its negative material.
      A. plurality; insulated
      B. idiom; singled
      C. idiosyncrasy; enumerated
      D. surplus; enumerated

Exercise IV. Complete the sentence by inferring information about the italicized word from its context.

1.   Freddy often *singled* out his favorite friend in order to…

2.   Al attempted to *enumerate* the many uses of a comma, but he…

3.   Edie was *nonplussed* after she fell clumsily, so her friends…

**Exercise V. Fill in the blank with the word from the Unit that best completes the sentence, using the root
      we supply as a clue. Then, answer the questions that follow the paragraphs.**

Who is your favorite professional athlete? Can you imagine him or her spying on enemy countries or fighting in a war? Can you imagine your favorite star sneaking out at night, getting information about enemy positions and weapons, and then sneaking back into the team hotel?

This sounds like the plot for a movie, but it isn't—it is the real-life story of Moe Berg. He started life as the child of poor Russian immigrants, and ended up with the offer of a Medal of Freedom from the United States government, following a fourteen-year major league baseball career that involved some unusual adventures.

Despite his poor beginnings, Berg soon rose beyond the expectations of most of his social class. He excelled in baseball; his high school team won eighteen consecutive games during his senior year, and he was admitted to Princeton University, where he began the study of seven languages. After graduating, he continued both baseball and academics; he made the Brooklyn Robins (later the Dodgers) as a backup catcher in 1923, and, during the off-season, he continued studying languages in Paris and at New York City's Columbia University. His solitary lifestyle, however, combined with his habit of appearing, disappearing, and staying in isolation, made him few friends.

Moe Berg began attracting the interest of agencies outside baseball. In 1934, an American all-star team was selected to tour Japan. Alongside such great hitters as Babe Ruth, Lou Gehrig, and Jimmie Foxx, Berg was chosen to make the trip. Because he knew a great deal about Japanese language and culture, Berg was a favorite of the Japanese public and press. However, he had a _____ (SING) purpose, different from the other ballplayers: he filmed the military installations, shipyards, and industrial plants in Tokyo from the top of a hospital during the team's stay. These films were eventually used when the United States planned its raids on mainland Japan near the end of World War II.

Berg left baseball in 1937 and joined the Office of Strategic Services, which later became the CIA. During World War II, he performed _____ (NUM) missions as a spy. The most dramatic came in December, 1944, when he attended a lecture given by Germany's premier nuclear physicist to find out the status of Germany's atomic weapons program. If enough progress had been made to pose a threat to the United States, Berg was to shoot the scientist and then swallow a cyanide tablet. Fortunately for the United States and for Berg, Germany was not close to creating even a single nuclear weapon, and Berg returned to his hotel.

In our own time, it may be hard to imagine a professional athlete having such diversity of talent and knowledge, but such a combination was found in Moe Berg.

1.   The writing style of this essay could best be described as
      A. persuasive.
      B. descriptive.
      C. argumentative.
      D. informative.

2.   With which of the following statements would the author most likely agree?
      A. Most professional athletes would not be able to handle the challenges of being a spy.
      B. Moe Berg contributed significantly to the Allied victory in World War I.
      C. If Moe Berg had spent more time studying languages, he would have been more helpful as a spy.
      D. Princeton University normally did not accept poor students.

3.   Which inference is supported by this essay?
      A. Pitchers generally require a lot of development to be successful spies.
      B. Defense requires more thought than offense in baseball.
      C. Catchers need to be able to hit very well to make a team.
      D. The United States suspected Japan's motives well before the War.

4.   What would be the best title for this essay?
      A. Why the United States Won World War II
      B. A History of Spies in Sports
      C. Moe Berg
      D. A Catcher's Spy Secrets

**Exercise VI. Drawing on your knowledge of roots and words in context, read the following selection and
      define the *italicized* words. If you cannot figure out the meaning of the words on your own, look
      them up in a dictionary. Note that *super* means "above."**

Although Conni was only a *supernumerary*, she was excited by her first role in a real Broadway play. She
was in a group of extras who the director told to stroll around the "picnic grounds" of the opening scene. When
the lead actor entered, however, Conni strolled towards him and bowed as she passed. She hoped that this one
scene would hint that she is an actress of *pluralistic* talent. Given the opportunity, she could play a variety of
different roles.

UNIT NINE

MENT

Latin MENS, MENTIS, "mind"

DEMENTED   (də mən´ təd)   *adj.*   Out of one's mind; insane
L. de, "out of," + mentis = *out of one's mind*
The filmmaker insisted that his movies made sense, but to many people, what he
did seemed completely *demented*.
syn: crazy   *ant*: sane

MENTALITY   (men tal´ ə tē)   *n.*   State of mind
Al's vicious *mentality* led him to launch attacks on many of his former friends.

MNE

Greek MIMNESKEIN, "to remember"
MNEMOS, "remembering"

AMNESTY   (am´ nes tē)   *n.*   Pardon for offenses
G. a, "not," + mimneskein = *not remembering*
During the general *amnesty*, Ted was released from the government prison.
syn: absolution

MNEMONIC   (nē mon´ ək)   *adj.*   Aiding in memory
Many educational professionals encourage students to use *mnemonic* devices
when studying for tests.

GNO

Greek GIGNOSKEIN, "to know"

III In order to diagnose a problem, you must be able to set apart (dia) what needs to be analyzed. Unless you can logically group and order these parts, you will not be able to understand the trouble.

DIAGNOSIS   (dī əg nō´ səs)   *n.*   Statement naming the cause of a condition
G. dia, "apart," + gignoskein = *to know apart*
After doctors had performed numerous tests on the patient, they decided upon a
diagnosis.
syn: identification

PROGNOSIS   (prog nō´ səs)   *n.*   Expectation of the way something will turn
        out; prediction
G. pro, "before" + gignoskein = *to know before*
Because Marie was in excellent physical condition, her *prognosis* for beating the
disease was very good.
syn: prediction

NOT, NOISS, NAISS
Latin NOSCERE, NOTUM, "to know"

NOTORIOUS (nō tôr´ ē əs) *adj.*   Famous in a negative way
Betsy was *notorious* for planning huge parties and then canceling them at the last minute.
syn: infamous

CONNOISSEUR (kon ə sōōr´) *n.*   One who is knowledgeable about a subject
Chef Rodrigo was a *connoisseur* of shellfish, having traveled the world to taste them all.

RECONNAISSANCE(rē kon´ ə səns) *n.*   Exploration to gain knowledge or information
The lieutenant accompanied his men on a *reconnaissance* maneuver, during which they spotted several enemy tents.

RATIO
Latin RATIO, RATIONIS, "reason"

RATION (ra´ shən) *v.*   To divide and distribute evenly
In order to prolong her experience of the excellent novel, Sylvia *rationed* the number of pages she read each day.
syn: divide

RATIONAL (ra´ shən əl) *adj.*   Sound in mind; logical
Although Samantha tried to be *rational* about losing her dog, she felt that she would go crazy with worry.
syn: sensible

It's important to make the RATIONS RATIONAL.

▥ *Both* connoisseur *and* reconnaissance *come to English from French. One French word meaning "to know" is* conoistre, *from cognoscere (co, "very," + gnoscere = "to know very well"). From it, we get* connoisseur. *The French for "recognize" is* reconoistre, *from* recognoscere *("to know well again"), and from this word, we get* reconnaissance.

EXERCISES - UNIT NINE

Exercise I. Complete the sentence in a way that shows you understand the meaning of the italicized vocabulary word.

1.   Sailors on the long journey from Russia to America *rationed* their food so that…

2.   Dirk usually made very *rational* decisions, so we were surprised when he…

3.   Many people in the audience at the circus wondered whether Ray was *demented* when he…

4.   The whole *mentality* of the staff at the restaurant changed when…

5.   Those who had participated in the failed uprising were given *amnesty* only if they…

6.   Gretchen employed various *mnemonic* techniques to help her…

7.   The train robber was so *notorious* for violent holdups that…

8.   As a *connoisseur* of classic cars, Michelle was able to spot…

9.   When the soldiers sent on the *reconnaissance* mission did not return, we feared that…

10. We found that the allergist's *diagnosis* was incorrect when…

11. Although the *prognosis* for the town's economy was bad, many hoped that…

Exercise II. Fill in the blank with the best word from the choices below. One word will not be used.

       rational   ration   demented   amnesty

1.   Failure to appropriately _____ out the surplus money in the treasury will result in budget problems next year.

2.   The political activist preferred to die rather that accept a(n) _____ from a government he considered corrupt and murderous.

3.   We often wonder what kind of _____ mind would dream up some of the programs currently on television.

Fill in the blank with the best word from the choices below. One word will not be used.

mnemonic   connoisseur   prognosis   notorious   diagnosis

4.   Though Erica considered herself a _____ of comic books, her actual collection was very small.

5.   Doctors noted that the _____ of the disease for a nonsmoking man was better than for a smoker.

6.   Rhyme can be a powerful _____ tool, but it can also cause students to lose sight of what they are learning.

7.   The _____ murderer had struck again, leaving his trademark clue at the scene of the crime.

Fill in the blank with the best word from the choices below. One word will not be used.

reconnaissance   rational   prognosis   mentality   diagnosis

8.   Kat's paranoid _____ led her to suspect even her close friends of betrayal.

9.   Families traveling to California by wagon often sent out a scout to do some _____.

10.   We found that Joseph's _____ of the root cause of the tax mess was very accurate.

11.   The dean urged the rioting students to be _____ and think twice before taking any drastic action.

Exercise III. Choose the set of words that best completes the sentence.

1.   Unless we carefully _____ out our funds for the next few months, the _____ for our investment club is not very good.
     A.   diagnose; connoisseur
     B.   ration; reconnaissance
     C.   diagnose; mentality
     D.   ration; prognosis

2.   Although the leader of the rebel forces was _____ for her violence and destructive tendencies, she was granted a(n) _____ by the ruling Prime Minister.
     A.   rational; connoisseur
     B.   notorious; amnesty
     C.   demented; prognosis
     D.   mnemonic; amnesty

3.   Does there appear to be a _____ cause for the horrible crime, or was the person who committed it truly _____?
     A.   rational; demented
     B.   notorious; mnemonic
     C.   demented; rational
     D.   notorious; rational

4. Because he had been a(n) _____ of fine cheeses for many years, Richard appeared to have a rather snobbish _____.
   A. amnesty; mentality
   B. mentality; diagnosis
   C. reconnaissance; prognosis
   D. connoisseur; mentality

5. When the two army scouts developed a strange disease after they returned from their _____ mission, they asked the company medic for a(n) _____.
   A. reconnaissance; diagnosis
   B. demented; prognosis
   C. rational; amnesty
   D. amnesty; prognosis

Exercise IV. Complete the sentence by inferring information about the italicized word from its context.

1. The fashion reviewer and *connoisseur* wrote that jeans…

2. If Gail used a *mnemonic* technique to learn musical scales, we can assume she has to…

3. If the man with stomach cancer is given a good *prognosis* by the doctor, he will probably…

Exercise V. Fill in the blank with the word from the Unit that best completes the sentence, using the root we supply as a clue. Then, answer the questions that follow the paragraphs.

Aron Ralston is a mountain climber who finds emotional escape hiking in treacherous environments. On April 26, 2003, however, he was literally stopped in his tracks when he became pinned by an eight-hundred-pound boulder. Ralston knew a(n) _____ (NAISS) mission to find him wasn't likely, since he'd told no one of his plans to hike for the day in Utah's Blue John Canyon. He figured there were three choices left to him: moving the boulder with his climbing gear, chipping away at the rock, or cutting off his arm with his pocketknife. Although he did think about having his cremated ashes scattered on the mountain where his family had climbed together, he decided dying was not an alternative.

It was a Saturday afternoon when the twenty-seven year-old Ralston became pinned. He tried rigging a series of pulleys to move the boulder, and he tried chipping away at it with his pocketknife, but neither attempt worked. By Tuesday, he had run out of water. He had licked clean the wrappers of four candy bars he had enjoyed on his way to the canyon and eaten the only other _____ (RAT) he had brought with him: two burritos. He knew if he stayed there he would die. He also knew no one might ever find his body, which most likely would be washed away by flash floods in the canyon. Ralston knew that to save his own life he would have to do the unimaginable: amputate his own arm. By day five, after sharpening his knife, he said, "Basically, I got my surgical table ready." He used a tourniquet, his bike shorts for padding, and the cheap multi-tool knife he carried. Then he bravely went to work and operated on himself. The whole process took about an hour.

Ralston's energy didn't fail him once he finished, either. After freeing himself and leaving half his arm behind, he crawled through the canyon, used a rope to get down a sixty-foot cliff, and then walked about five miles before encountering other hikers, who gave him water and two Oreo cookies. After walking a few more miles, Ralston and his rescuers were spotted and rescued by a Utah Public Safely Helicopter. The pilot was hoping Ralston wouldn't pass out on the way to the hospital. On the contrary, though, he talked to the deputies in the helicopter. "When he landed at the hospital," the pilot said, "he got up and walked right into the emergency room." Ralston underwent surgery to close his wound in preparation for a prosthetic arm, and his _____ (GNO) is very good. Ralston still plans to climb mountains. In fact, he wants to become the first person to climb fifty-five of Colorado's highest peaks in winter. From now on, however, he says he'll tell people where he's going.

1. Why do you think Ralston hiked the canyon as he did?
    A. It was just a one-day hike.
    B. He didn't think anything was going to happen.
    C. He had hiked alone before.
    D. All of the above.

2. The only food Ralston had while pinned to the rock was
    A. four candy bars.
    B. two Oreo cookies.
    C. two burritos.
    D. All of the above.

3. The best title for this essay would be
    A. How to Save Yourself.
    B. Survival through Determination and Courage.
    C. Never Walk Alone.
    D. Be Prepared.

4. Ralston
    A. decided he didn't want to die.
    B. knew he could kill himself.
    C. considered starting a fire.
    D. All of the above.

Exercise VI. Drawing on your knowledge of roots and words in context, read the following selection and define the *italicized* words. If you cannot figure out the meaning of the words on your own, look them up in a dictionary. Note that *a* means "not, without."

Although the president of Marzipan Creations has tried to *rationalize* some of the decisions she made on behalf of the corporate stockholders, she can hardly excuse putting personal items on her expense account. Accountants looking carefully at the books have found that her nephew's college education as well as a speedboat and three prize thoroughbreds were paid for by the company. Unless she is a certified *amnesiac*, however, there is no way the C.E.O. could have forgotten buying these things.

UNIT TEN

JURIS
Latin IUS, IURIS, "law"

JURISPRUDENCE (jŏŏr is prōō´ dəns) *n.* Study or science of law
L. juris, "law," + prudentia, "knowledge" = *knowledge of law*
Carol's understanding of *jurisprudence* was valuable when I was writing a book on the legal system.

JURISDICTION (jŏŏr is dik´ shən) *n.* Area of influence
Although the tax official lives in Chester County, cases from all over the state fall within his *jurisdiction*.

PERJURE (per´ jər) *v.* To lie under oath
L. per, "wrong," + juris = *to wrong the law*
Though Janice argued that she had given the court wrong information by accident, the defense attorney said she had *perjured* herself.

▣ Jurisdiction *is the right to speak (diction) the law (juris) in a particular area.*

PUN
Latin PUNIRE, PUNITUM, "to punish"
POENA, "punishment, penalty"

IMPUNITY (im pū´ nə tē) *n.* Freedom from punishment
L. in, "not," + punire = *not punished*
Because the store owner was almost blind, Kelly stole candy with *impunity*.

PUNITIVE (pū´ nə tiv) *adj.* Intended to punish; penalizing
The *punitive* fine I received for speeding convinced me never to go above seventy miles an hour again.

SUBPOENA (sub pē´ nə) *n.* A legal document summoning someone to court
L. sub, "beneath," + poena = *under penalty* (of law)
Though Keith received a *subpoena* in the mail, he refused to appear in court.

LITI
Latin LITIGARE, LITIGATUM, "to press a lawsuit"

LITIGATION   (lit ə gā´ shən)   *n.*   The process of a lawsuit
Roger was told that unless he paid his bill immediately, the company would begin *litigation* against him.

LITIGANT   (lit´ ə gənt)   *n.*   Someone involved in a lawsuit
As one of several *litigants* in a case against a major car company, Anne had to give testimony about the accident she had been in.

NOM, NEM
Greek NOMOS, "law, custom, share"
NEMEIN, "to measure out"

AUTONOMOUS   (aw ton´ ə məs)   *adj.*   Self-governing; independent
G. autos, "self," + nomos = *self-law*
Starting next year, the territory will become an *autonomous* nation, complete with its own government, laws, and army.

NEMESIS   (nem´ ə səs)   *n.*   Something causing pain or harm; enemy
Tim secretly hoped that Lily, his *nemesis*, would eventually become his best friend.

DIC
Greek DIKE, "justice"

SYNDICATE   (sin´ də kit)   *n.*   A gathering of people with a common interest
G. syn, "together," + dike = *justice together*
In order to have more power in their fight against the company, union members formed a *syndicate*.

▣ *The Greek goddess* Nemesis *was said to measure out vengeance or justice against individuals. In modern English, however, a* nemesis *is simply an enemy.*

CINDY and KATE combined their lemonade stands into a SYNDICATE.

EXERCISES - UNIT TEN

Exercise I. Complete the sentence in a way that shows you understand the meaning of the italicized vocabulary word.

1.   Leila recognized the man being interviewed as a *litigant* from…

2.   The surgeon read up on *jurisprudence* when she was called to…

3.   The *syndicate* of businessmen consisted of…

4.   The children broke rules with *impunity* because their parents…

5.   One of the *punitive* measures the state has taken against shoplifters is…

6.   Managers at the company tried to persuade clients against *litigation* because…

7.   The province has finally become *autonomous*, but for many years before was…

8.   Marla started to consider the mail carrier her *nemesis* when…

9.   Ralph was in danger of *perjuring* himself when he told the court that…

10.   Because the power to prosecute the crime fell under the *jurisdiction* of the town of Greenville…

11.   When Sandy received his *subpoena*, he knew he would have to…

Exercise II. Fill in the blank with the best word from the choices below. One word will not be used.

litigant   punitive   nemesis   impunity

1.   I did not expect my old high school _____ to appear at my party, since we still did not get along.

2.   The speed at which Warren drives indicates that he feels he has _____ from the police.

3.   Although the smoking ban seems _____ to some, it was actually designed to help us all.

Fill in the blank with the best word from the choices below. One word will not be used.

autonomous   syndicate   jurisprudence   jurisdiction   litigants

4.   In a class-action lawsuit, there can be dozens or even hundreds of _____.

5.   The partners split up their company, with each setting up a(n) _____ bank account.

6.   The powerful _____ of film directors had total control over every movie released by the studio.

7.   Justin's years of studying _____ made him an ideal candidate for district judge.

Fill in the blank with the best word from the choices below. One word will not be used.

litigation   syndicate   subpoena   jurisdiction   perjure

8.   For ignoring the _____, Katie and Lucy were charged with contempt of court.

9.   The governor reminded everyone that a sheriff's _____ did not extend beyond the boundary of the county.

10.   The person injured in the car accident started _____ against the other driver.

11.   Though Milla knew she would _____ herself, she decided she would lie about where she had been the night of the accident.

Exercise III. Choose the set of words that best completes the sentence.

1.   While some members of the food _____ wished to pursue _____ against the company, most group managers wished for a quiet settlement of the dispute.
    A. autonomous; subpoena
    B. syndicate; litigation
    C. syndicate; impunity
    D. nemesis; litigant

2.   The lawyer warned his client that severe _____ action would be taken against her if she _____ herself on the stand.
    A. litigation; syndicated
    B. autonomous; litigated
    C. punitive; perjured
    D. autonomous; syndicated

3.   Even though the country became legally _____ after it won independence, certain crimes committed there fell under the _____ of the previous rulers' court.
    A. autonomous; jurisdiction
    B. punitive; jurisprudence
    C. litigated; subpoena
    D. punitive; jurisdiction

4. As the main _____ in a civil case, I was able to issue a(n) _____ to several witnesses who would back up my story.
   A. nemesis; impunity
   B. litigation; autonomous
   C. jurisprudence; impunity
   D. litigant; subpoena

5. Though Bessie was Arnold's _____, and he longed to make a fool of her, he knew that he could not tease her with _____ because of her temper.
   A. litigant; nemesis
   B. jurisprudence; subpoena
   C. nemesis; impunity
   D. impunity; litigant

Exercise IV. Complete the sentence by inferring information about the italicized word from its context.

1. Norman complained, "Math is my *nemesis,* and I just cannot..."

2. If the defendant *perjures* himself at the trial, the judge will likely...

3. When Marisól received the court *subpoena,* she was worried because...

Exercise V. Fill in the blank with the word from the Unit that best completes the sentence, using the root we supply as a clue. Then, answer the questions that follow the paragraphs.

The historical, social, and cultural significance of Lewis and Clark's expedition is remarkable. Their journey marks the onset of the Westward expansion of the U.S., when a large number of Americans began to travel and settle west of the Mississippi River. It also laid to rest the American dream of finding a Northwest Passage, a waterway that was supposed to link the Atlantic to the Pacific Ocean. The goals assigned to the group of explorers, also called the Corps of Discovery, were to map the new territory, to note the animal and plant life they encountered for both scientific and commercial purposes, and document Indian cultures. However, the group was also sent as a representative of the U.S. government. Its diplomatic purpose was to inform the Indian people living on the land acquired in the Louisiana Purchase of the new _____ (JURIS) under which their land fell. Lewis and Clark promised the Native Americans military protection, trade benefits, and semi- _____ (NOM) government in exchange for peace.

The Corps of Discovery experienced great success in maintaining peaceful relationships during their journey west. The first group of Native Americans they met were the Missouri and Oto tribes. Clark warned his crew to be on guard, but their conference went smoothly, and the peace pipe was smoked, indicating both parties' good intentions. Lewis and Clark provided gifts to the tribes, such as medals, cloth, and gunpowder, as a sign of appreciation for peace and cooperation. Subsequent meetings with other tribes went equally well. Always beneficial to Lewis and Clark's group to show it was coming in peace was the presence of Sacagawea, the Native American woman traveling with them. She was able to act as a guide in the areas of the Shoshoni, which the expedition entered in the fall of 1805.

Despite the widespread, peaceful welcoming of the Corps of Discovery, the travelers did have one violent encounter with a group of Blackfeet near the Missouri River on the way back to Washington. The corps had split, with Clark and a few men exploring south, along the Yellowstone River, and Lewis with some men heading north. The hostile group attempted to take Lewis and his men's weapons and horses. One Native American was shot and another stabbed in the conflict. These were the only fatalities known during the entire journey. While providing the United States government with excellent maps and information on its newly acquired land, the Corps of Discovery is also notable for laying a foundation for positive relations with the Native American population.

1. How did the presence of Sacagawea benefit the Corps of Discovery?
    A. She took care of their children.
    B. She cooked for the men.
    C. She acted as a guide.
    D. She found their lost medical supplies.

2. What would be an appropriate title for this passage?
    A. Lewis and Clark Map America
    B. Sacagawea Helps the Corps of Discovery
    C. Violence on the Lewis and Clark Trip
    D. Lewis and Clark's Relationship with the Native Americans

3. What is the main idea of this passage?
    A. Lewis and Clark had a violent encounter with the Blackfeet.
    B. One purpose of the trip was to pass along information to whomever the Corps encountered.
    C. The Indians appreciated the presence of Sacagawea.
    D. Lewis and Clark got along with the Native Americans.

4. Which President sent the Corps of Discovery out?
    A. Lincoln
    B. Washington
    C. Adams
    D. The article does not specify.

Exercise VI. Drawing on your knowledge of roots and words in context, read the following selection and define the *italicized* words. If you cannot figure out the meaning of the words on your own, look them up in a dictionary. Note that *consult* means "one skilled in" and *a* means "no, none."

Even the most learned *jurisconsult* was at a loss when it came to explaining the strictness of laws regarding impeachment in the colonial government. Professor Ricardo Cain, who had spent fifty years of a distinguished legal career closely analyzing the colony's court system, and who had written numerous heavy volumes on the subject, said simply that the impeachment laws were written at a time when the colony was in a state of *anomie*. Fearing that, without harsh laws and punishments, a dictator would take advantage of the chaos and lawlessness raging in the area, the colony's rulers had decided to make impeachment a severe and permanent process.

UNIT ELEVEN

VET
Latin VETUS, VETERIS "old"

While a veteran can be anyone who has spent many years in a particular field or occupation, the word often describes someone who has served in the military.

VETERAN (vet´ ər ən) *n.* Someone very experienced in something; expert
Sarah, a *veteran* watcher of TV news programs, auditioned for the new quiz show about current events.
syn: professional   *ant:* novice

INVETERATE (in vet´ ər ət) *adj.* Having done something for a long time; habitual
L. in, "in," + veteris = *in the old*
Terrance was an *inveterate* gambler, and his wife finally divorced him because of it.
syn: practiced

FREQ
Latin FREQUENS, "frequent, numerous"

FREQUENT (frē´ kwent) *v.* To visit often or repeatedly
When I travel overseas, I always *frequent* local restaurants, rather than fast food places.
syn: patronize   *ant:* avoid

INFREQUENT (in frē´ kwent) *adj.* Not occurring often
L. in, "not," + frequens = *not frequent*
The two-year-long drought was broken only by *infrequent* small showers.
syn: rare   *ant:* habitual

ANN
Latin ANNUS, "year"

ANNALS (a´ nəls) *n.* A record of something; a history
Nowhere in the *annals* of the town was there mention of the shooting, so we assumed that the story was false.
syn: archives

ANNUITY (a nōō´ ə tē) *n.* Payment received every year
My mom's *annuity* amounted to over a million dollars, but it was set aside only for her grandchildren.

ANNUAL (an´ ū əl) *adj.* Occurring every year
When the longest day of the year arrived, many ancient civilizations celebrated the *annual* planting of crops.
syn: yearly

CHRON
Greek KRONOS, "time"

CHRONOLOGY (kron ol´ ə jē) *n.* A history arranged by time
The police wanted to know the *chronology* of the events that occurred just before the car wreck.

CHRONIC (kron´ ik) *adj.* Happening repeatedly or over a long period of time
Even though Cory has a *chronic* cough, he refuses to visit a doctor.
syn: constant   *ant:* sporadic

TEMP
Latin TEMPUS, TEMPORIS, "time"

CONTEMPORANEOUS (kən tem pər a´ nē əs) *adj.* Happening at or around the
            same time
L. con, "together," + temporis = *together in time*
The Russian Revolution and World War I were *contemporaneous* events that occurred in the early years of the 20th century.
syn: coexisting, simultaneous

CONTEMPORARY (kən tem´ pər ər ē) *n.* A person from the same time period
            or generation
One *contemporary* of Abe Lincoln was the ex-slave Frederick Douglass, who eventually met the President.

TEMPO (tem´ pō) *n.* Rhythm or beat
Using only his baton, the conductor instructed the orchestra to increase the *tempo* of the music.

> **Ⅲ** A crony (*from* kronos) is a friend or associate whom you have known a long time.

The conductor upped the TEMPO when he lost his TEMPER.

EXERCISES - UNIT ELEVEN

Exercise I. Complete the sentence in a way that shows you understand the meaning of the italicized vocabulary word.

1.   When the *tempo* of the music changed, the dancers in the club...

2.   For an *inveterate* shoplifter like Ashley, the future seems likely to bring...

3.   Charles stopped receiving his *annuity* from the oil company when...

4.   A *chronology* of the war provided information about...

5.   The Spanish painter was not a *contemporary* of the Italian sculptor, but...

6.   Because the years in which the swimmer was at her peak were *contemporaneous* with a major war in her country...

7.   Because he was a *veteran* of the movie industry, Don was often asked to...

8.   Because there was no record of a flood like this in the *annals* of the town's history...

9.   The Dineesons *frequent* the shops and restaurants of the city's East Side because...

10.   In order to prepare for the *annual* picnic, the company needs...

11.   Though Claudette's visits to the park had been *infrequent*, she now...

12.   Facing a *chronic* shortage of medical supplies, the hospital...

Exercise II. Fill in the blank with the best word from the choices below. One word will not be used.

inveterate   chronic   annuity   infrequent   veteran

1.   My grandmother is a(n) _____ customer at the beauty salon because she finds the long walk there very tiring.

2.   It is especially difficult for a(n) _____ smoker like Chip to give up the habit.

3.   Annoyed by the _____ pain in his feet, Stanley finally decided to see a doctor.

4.   As a(n) _____ of the downtown art scene, Linda knew all of the painters and sculptors in the area.

Fill in the blank with the best word from the choices below. One word will not be used.

annual   tempo   annuity   contemporary   annals

5.   Although the painter was not a(n) _____ of Picasso, their styles are very similar.

6.   Jake is retired, but continues to receive a(n) _____ from the stock he purchased as an employee.

7.   The marchers proceeded down the street in the same _____as the drummer.

8.   In the _____of the Medical Society, there are several instances of this strange and deadly disease.

Fill in the blank with the best word from the choices below. One word will not be used.

chronology   veteran   contemporaneous   frequented   annual

9.   The period during which the small mammals wandered the Earth was _____with the reign of the dinosaurs.

10.   The parade of ships was not a(n) _____event, but one that occurred every ten years.

11.   Investigators will not be able to solve the case until they have a reliable _____of the years in which the crimes were committed.

12.   Neighborhood kids _____ Isaiah's Ice Cream Parlor until a kitchen fire forced it to close.

Exercise III. Choose the set of words that best completes the sentence.

1.   Although Josie was a(n) _____ of the news industry, she was a(n) _____ visitor to the press club where many reporters liked to gather.
A.   veteran; contemporaneous
B.   contemporary; annual
C.   annals; frequent
D.   veteran; infrequent

2.   Because Patsy was a(n) _____ smoker, she soon developed _____ lung problems.
A.   inveterate; chronic
B.   chronic; annual
C.   infrequent; contemporaneous
D.   frequent; inveterate

3.   Henry Ride, a(n) _____ of George Washington, was said to _____ the same businesses and theaters as the President.
A.   contemporary; inveterate
B.   annuity; inveterate
C.   contemporary; frequent
D.   tempo; frequent

4.   The _____ awards ceremony is usually _____ with the coming of autumn, but this year,
      it was delayed by a month.
      A.   inveterate; infrequent
      B.   contemporary; chronic
      C.   infrequent; annuity
      D.   annual; contemporaneous

5.   Because the _____ of the church are so mixed up, they do not provide an accurate _____
      of the events that took place.
      A.   contemporary; annals
      B.   annals; chronology
      C.   veterans; chronology
      D.   chronologies; veteran

Exercise IV. Complete the sentence by inferring information about the italicized word from its context.

1.   When Bill has to write down a *chronology* of his life, he will probably start with…

2.   If the musicians are confused by *tempo* of the piece, they may try to…

3.   If two people are called *contemporaries* of each other, we can assume…

**Exercise V. Fill in the blank with the word from the Unit that best completes the sentence, using the root
          we supply as a clue. Then, answer the questions that follow the paragraphs.**

When Europeans first came to the New World, they thought the native cultures there were not as well developed as their own. Nothing could have been further from the truth, however. One of the best examples of a highly developed Native American culture was that of the Aztecs of Mexico. Like the Europeans, the Aztecs had a detailed system of government, a written language, and strong religious beliefs. Their ability to design and engineer buildings was so advanced that they built their capital city, Tenochtitlan, in the middle of a lake.

The ancient Aztecs came from a place called Aztlan. Around the first millennium A.D., according to the _____(ANN) of their history, they received a message from one of their gods, Huitzilopochtli, who told them that they should search for a better place to live. Huitzilopochtli said that he would give the Aztecs a sign when they had come to the right place. He told them that when they saw an eagle standing alone and eating a snake, they would have found the place where he wanted them to build a great city. The Aztecs did as Huitzilopochtli said and traveled south, sojourning for many years in an area called Coatepec. Part of the original group's descendants eventually left Coatepec, though, after numerous religious disputes, and when they reached what is now central Mexico,

they saw the sign their god had given them. There, in the middle of a lake, stood an eagle eating a snake. The Aztecs knew this was the land that had been promised to them; consequently, regardless of the lake, they began building Tenochtitlan there.

The plan for Tenochtitlan was a lot like that of the European city of Venice—the rise of the two cities was _____ (TEMPOR)—although the Aztecs did not know that Europe even existed. Since Tenochtitlan was built on top of a lake, the main form of transportation was the canoe. Instead of streets, the city had canals. Transportation was not the only thing that the Aztec city had in common with Europe, though. Just like its cities, the Aztecs were ruled by a king, who was thought to be a relative of the gods. The Aztecs developed a system of writing, although it was based on pictures. There were people among the Aztecs who kept a _____ (CHRON) of the culture's history, births and deaths, records of taxes paid, and of land bought and sold. The Aztecs also had a strong religion. Not only were their kings thought to be descendants of gods, but the people in Aztec culture who were most admired were priests. The same could be said for European cultures.

When Cortes, the Spanish explorer, landed in Mexico in the early 1500's, he thought that the Aztecs could be easily defeated because they still used ancient weapons like spears and swords, while the Spanish forces had guns and cannons. The Aztecs put up a strong fight, however. When Cortes finally did capture their king, Montezuma, it marked the end of an intelligent and highly organized Native American culture.

1. Which of the following best presents the main idea of this essay?
   A. The Aztec culture had a lot in common with European cultures.
   B. The Aztecs built their capital city in the middle of a lake.
   C. The Aztecs traveled many years before settling down in Tenochtitlan.
   D. Montezuma was the leader of the Aztecs.

2. The god Huitzilopochtli told the Aztecs to look for a sign when they were searching for a new home. What was that sign?
   A. a lake
   B. a location in the center of what is now Mexico
   C. a certain type of snake
   D. an eagle eating a snake

3. Which of the following accomplishments can you infer was probably the most important to the continuation of the Aztec culture?
   A. having a king who was a descendant of the gods
   B. honoring their priests
   C. creating a system of writing
   D. using canoes to travel in their capital city

4. Today, the Mexican flag shows a picture of an eagle eating a snake. In light of the information given in this essay, why is that important?
   A. The eagle is a symbol of power.
   B. It honors Mexico's greatest native culture.
   C. It shows the strength of Mexico.
   D. Both the eagle and the snake are native to Mexico.

Exercise VI. Drawing on your knowledge of roots and words in context, read the following selection and define the *italicized* words. If you cannot figure out the meaning of the words on your own, look them up in a dictionary. Note that *super* means "over, very."

When the policemen knocked on the door of the large manor, they were greeted by a *superannuated* butler. The old fellow seemed barely able to hear, and it took some time to explain to him why they had come. Of course, it was really no butler at all, but Mr. Darcy in disguise. Mr. Darcy *temporized* while his criminal partner made a getaway from the back. When the police realized that he was stalling, they pushed past him into the house, but it was too late. Their prime suspect had escaped.

UNIT TWELVE

TER
Latin TERRERE, TERRITUM "to frighten, to scare"

TERRORIZE   (ter´ ər īz)   *v.*   To repeatedly frighten
That huge dog has *terrorized* the children in the neighborhood for much too long.
syn: alarm   *ant*: calm

DETER   (dē tər´)   *v.*   To prevent; to discourage
L. de, "away from," + terrere = *to scare away from*
Jessica tried everything to *deter* deer from eating her plants, but the only solution was to place a large fence around her garden.
syn: hinder   *ant*: encourage

HORR
Latin HORRERE, "to shudder, be afraid"

HORRIFIC   (hə rif´ ik)   *adj.*   Causing extreme horror or disgust
Seven cars were involved in the *horrific* accident that killed four of the drivers.
syn: awful   *ant*: pleasant

ABHOR   (ab hôr´)   *v.*   To feel horror towards; hate
L. ab, "from," + horrere = *to shudder away from*
Nellie *abhors* people who act like they are superior to their friends.
syn: despise   *ant*: love

III   *The verb* horrere *literally means "to tremble with fear so that one's hair stands on end." This is why the word* horrid, *which in modern English means "frightfully bad," appears in some older works of English literature meaning "bristling" or "shaggy."*

TREPID
Latin TREPIDUS, "afraid, disturbed"

TREPIDATION   (trep ə dā´ shən)   *n.*   State of fear or alarm
Aisha was filled with *trepidation* at the thought of her upcoming driver's examination.
syn: dread

INTREPID   (in trep´ əd)   *adj.*   Bold; unafraid
L. in, "not," + trepidus = *not afraid*
Greg, an *intrepid* pilot, frequently landed his small plane on extremely rough ground in unfamiliar countries.
syn: brave, courageous   *ant*: fearful

FORMID
Latin FORMIDARE, "to fear"

FORMIDABLE (fôr´ mid ə bəl) *adj.* Difficult to overcome; intimidating
Just looking up at the *formidable* mountain was enough to make some climbers change their minds.
syn: daunting   *ant*: simple

REV
Latin VERERI, "to fear, respect"

REVERE (rə vēr´) *v.* To hold in awe; worship
L. re, "back," + vereri = *to respect back*
You may dislike the painter, but Tammy *reveres* him.
syn: admire, respect   *ant*: despise

IRREVERENT (i rev´ ə rent) *adj.* Not showing proper respect
L. in, "not," + re, "back," + vereri = *not giving respect back*
During the funeral, James made some *irreverent* remarks, and the Rabbi frowned at him.

TIM
Latin TIMOR, "fear"

INTIMIDATE (in tim´ ə dāt) *v.* To threaten with harm; to frighten
L. in, "into," + timor = *to put fear into*
Our team was unable to *intimidate* the other school's football players because we were much smaller than they were.
syn: bully, scare

TIMOROUS (tim´ ə rəs) *adj.* Afraid of danger; timid
The little child was so *timorous* that she began crying when she saw the clown at the carnival.
syn: shy   *ant*: brave

Ⅲ *The word* reverend *means "deserving respect and admiration." It often appears in the title of an ordained Christian minister, as in* The Reverend Doctor Martin Luther King, Jr.

The TIMOROUS girl would not speak to TIM OR US.

EXERCISES - UNIT TWELVE

Exercise I. Complete the sentence in a way that shows you understand the meaning of the italicized vocabulary word.

1. Pauline approached the spelling bee with *trepidation* because...

2. Jeff knew that the opposing baseball team was *formidable* because...

3. Though Annie claims to *abhor* lying, she...

4. The basketball player tries to *intimidate* his opponents by...

5. The injuries suffered by the stuntman were so *horrific* that...

6. Many young musicians *revere* the guitarist because...

7. Dawn's *timorous* answer to the teacher's question showed that she felt...

8. If you want to *deter* ants from invading your kitchen cabinets,...

9. My little sister's *intrepid* nature has often led her to...

10. The *irreverent* tone of the magazine article prompted many readers to...

11. Mrs. Wilson thought the neighborhood boys were *terrorizing* her, but they...

Exercise II. Fill in the blank with the best word from the choices below. One word will not be used.

horrific	deterred	terrorized	intimidate

1. So that he would not _____ his youngest students, the teacher bent down to their level.

2. Images from the war may be published in the newspaper, as long as they are not too _____ or disturbing.

3. The mysterious illness that had _____ the town ceased to be so frightening once a vaccine was developed.

Fill in the blank with the best word from the choices below. One word will not be used.

irreverent intrepid timorous abhors formidable

4. Somehow, the comedian was able to make _____ jokes at the expense of respected politicians and never get in trouble for it.

5. When asked a question by the principal, the _____ little boy looked down at his feet and said nothing.

6. Sally _____ modern fashions, so she makes all of her own clothes by hand.

7. Although the obstacles facing Jim were _____, he learned to walk again and even ran in a marathon.

Fill in the blank with the best word from the choices below. One word will not be used.

trepidation deter timorous intrepid revered

8. The anxiety I felt preparing for the mountain climb was nothing compared to my _____ when I saw the mountain for the first time.

9. The _____ crew of the tiny ship braved dangers that would have scared off many other sailors.

10. Even the threat of severe punishment did not _____ Andrew from writing on the walls.

11. Some people considered the leader a murderous criminal, while others _____ him as a hero.

Exercise III. Choose the set of words that best completes the sentence.

1. Although the huge banana split _____ many people with weak appetites, some _____ diners have given it a try.
   A. reveres; timorous
   B. intimidates; intrepid
   C. abhors; irreverent
   D. terrorizes; horrific

2. It is true that I _____ the actor for his stunning performances in several recent films, but I also _____ his rude and cruel behavior offscreen.
   A. revere; terrorize
   B. terrorize; abhor
   C. abhor; revere
   D. revere; abhor

3.   Mandy is once again facing _____ competition in the track meet, but I am sure it will not _____ her from participating.
     A. timorous; deter
     B. formidable; deter
     C. formidable; abhor
     D. horrific; abhor

4.   Otto had nightmares about a(n) _____ monster that _____ local citizens and threatened to destroy the world.
     A. horrific; deterred
     B. timorous; deterred
     C. intrepid; abhorred
     D. horrific; terrorized

5.   Janice was usually bold and talkative rather than _____ and shy, but she clearly felt some _____ about speaking before such a large audience.
     A. timorous; trepidation
     B. intrepid; intimidation
     C. horrific; abhorrence
     D. intrepid; trepidation

Exercise IV. Complete the sentence by inferring information about the italicized word from its context.

1.   You might describe someone as *intrepid* if he or she…

2.   If Jennifer *abhors* doing the dishes, she should probably…

3.   To *deter* further accidents at the corner, police will most likely…

Exercise V. Fill in the blank with the word from the Unit that best completes the sentence, using the root we supply as a clue. Then, answer the questions that follow the paragraphs.

Terrorism is any _____(HORR) and illegal act committed by a government or by private individuals to promote a political agenda. Terrorists use violence to _____ (TIM) whomever they oppose. And their methods date back to long before out own times. Throughout history, there have been those who lived by the sword and sought to _____(TER) innocent people for power or money.

Ancient Rome had to deal with German tribes, which the Romans called "barbarians," invading the perimeter of the Empire. In 267, the Goths, a large Germanic tribe from the area that is now Scandinavia, crossed the border of the Roman Empire around the Danube river. Eventually, the Romans were forced to evacuate the nearby provinces. Of course, Roman politicians themselves were involved in terrorism when they overthrew their own government by violent means.

In the Middle Ages, Europeans lived in fear of Vikings descending from Scandinavia. The Vikings were not seeking political power, though; they wanted the wealth of coastal villages. In order to obtain this plunder, they took to ships and traveled great distances.

In more recent centuries, pirates exploited the high seas, robbing merchant ships and passengers and raiding coastal villages for profit. In spite of the romantic image of pirates portrayed in Robert Louis Stevenson's character of Long John Silver in *Treasure Island*, pirates were brutal. They exploited the timid and weak. They waged a semi-war on whomever they chose to terrify, rob, or murder, without respect to any nation's flag, unless a king or queen paid the annual "tribute" to _____(TER) crime. In 1795, the United States government agreed to pay one million dollars to the Barbary pirates, who had been preying upon American shipping in the Mediterranean Sea. An annual payment was made until 1815, when the United States Navy, under Captain Stephen Decatur, won several sea battles in the Mediterranean, compelling the pirates to sign a peace treaty and putting an end to the harassment of American ships and the annual tribute.

Today, governments publicly claim not to negotiate with terrorists, and few governments will admit to using violence and terrorism against other nations. However, terrorism is still employed by many individuals and groups. Whether their motive is political or monetary, terrorists will exist as long as there are groups of people who feel they can use force as a weapon.

1.   What ended the attacks by pirates on American ships?
      A. the payment of one million dollars to the Barbary pirates
      B. a peace treaty signed in 1815
      C. the annual tribute paid by Captain Stephen Decatur
      D. respect for the American flag

2.   The author of the passage says that terrorism can be committed by
      A. individuals only.
      B. individuals and governments.
      C. governments only.
      D. pirates only.

3.   According to the passage, most terrorists want
      A. peace.
      B. religious freedom.
      C. nothing.
      D. power or money.

Exercise VI. Drawing on your knowledge of roots and words in context, read the following selection and define the *italicized* words. If you cannot figure out the meaning of the words on your own, look them up in a dictionary.

Darlene was a *trepid* tourist at first, afraid to stray too far from her group or her hotel. Soon enough, though, she realized that her fear was preventing her from seeing everything London had to offer. On Monday, therefore, she set out on her own, armed with a map and a camera. Her wanderings through the streets of the old city eventually led her to St. Paul's Cathedral. There, with visitors and pilgrims from all over the world, she stood in *reverential* silence, paying respect and honor to the history and the people for which the cathedral stood.

UNIT THIRTEEN

SPECT, SPIC
Latin SPICERE, SPECTUM, "to see"

SUSPECT (sus´pekt) *adj.* Not able to be trusted; suspicious
L. sub, "from beneath," + spectum = *looked at from beneath*
When scientists put the *suspect* theory to test, they found that it couldn't possibly be true.
syn: doubtful   *ant*: certain

CONSPICUOUS (kən spik´ū əs) *adj.* Standing out; unusual
L. con, "very," + spectum = *seen very much*
Everyone at the party could tell when Jerry arrived because of his high-pitched, *conspicuous* laughter.
syn: obvious

RESPECTIVE (rə spek´tiv) *adj.* Corresponding to each person or thing in a
          series
L. re, "back," + spectum = *looked back at, considered*
The substitute teacher became confused and made all students return to their *respective* seats.
syn: particular

DESPICABLE (de spik´ə bəl) *adj.* Deserving of hatred or disgust
L. de, "down," + spicere = *looked down upon*
The *despicable* crime at the local church prompted the entire community to band together to catch the suspect.
syn: vile   *ant*: likable

TUT, TUI
Latin TUERI, TUTUS, "to guard, watch over, look at"

TUTELAGE (tōōt´ə ləj) *n.* Instruction and guardianship
Under the professor's *tutelage* and guidance, Mary was able to finish her research and write the paper in less than six months.
syn: education

INTUITIVE (in tōō´ə tiv) *adj.* Understood without logic or rational
          knowledge
L. in, "on," + tueri = *to look on*
Sharon tried out for the starring role in the play because she had an *intuitive* sense that she would be perfect for the part.

III *The word* respect *means "appreciation or admiration," but it also means a particular quality or "side of something." This second meaning gives us* respective, *which means "particular or individual."*

OCUL
Latin OCULUS, "eye"

OCULAR (ok´ yə lər) *adj.*   Having to do with the eye
The boxer's *ocular* nerve became damaged after he received five punches to his face.

INOCULATE (in ok´ yə lāt) *v.*   To protect against disease, error or harm
The President's policy is to require all hospital workers to be *inoculated* against the most contagious diseases.

VIS, VID
Latin VIDERE, VISUM, "to see, to look at"

ADVISABLE   (ad vīz´ ə bəl) *adj.*   Appropriate to do; sensible
L. ad, "towards," + visum = *towards what seems (right)*
It is *advisable* to have a friend read over your essay for mistakes before you hand it to the teacher.

REVISE (rē vīz´) *v.*   To make corrections to; edit or redo
L. re, "again," + visum = *to look at again*
Mother had to *revise* the rules in our house when it became clear that they were too strict.

EVIDENT (ev´ ə dent) *adj.*   Clearly visible; obvious
L. e, "from," + videre = *from what can be seen*
It was certainly *evident* to Sheila that the correct answer was Christopher Columbus, but few people in the class agreed.
syn: plain, apparent

VISTA (vis´ tə) *n.*   A broad view; outlook
From the mountaintop, we had a perfect *vista* of over one hundred lakes spread out in every direction.

"Hey, MISTA, you're blocking my VISTA!"

An oculus is *not only an eye, but something eye-shaped, like the bud of a tree. To inoculate (in, "onto," + oculus, "bud") originally meant "to graft a bud from one tree onto another." We now use it to mean "introduce one substance into another to protect from harm" or even just "protect." The doctor inoculates you with a vaccine so that you don't get measles.*

EXERCISES - UNIT THIRTEEN

Exercise I. Complete the sentence in a way that shows you understand the meaning of the italicized vocabulary word.

1.   When Sam's *ocular* muscle was damaged, he began having difficulty…

2.   The actions of the police in the arrest of the local woman were so *despicable* that…

3.   The Census Bureau was forced to *revise* its information on the U.S. population when…

4.   My mother's *intuitive* understanding of her children's emotions allowed her to…

5.   Everything Debbie has told us about her college education is *suspect* because…

6.   Under the *tutelage* of the famous violin teacher, Tanya was able to…

7.   We matched the sweaters left in the classroom to their *respective* owners by…

8.   The accountant informed his client that a move out of the country would be *advisable* because…

9.   The hotel promised a stunning *vista*, but all we could see were…

10.   Because Lin was not *inoculated* against measles as a baby, she…

11.   Greg's absence from class that day was *conspicuous* because…

12.   The terrible damage done by the tornado became *evident* when…

Exercise II. Fill in the blank with the best word from the choices below. One word will not be used.

> inoculated   revised   vista   conspicuous   tutelage

1.   When we got to the top of the hill, we had a breathtaking _____ of the harbor.

2.   Gerard's bright orange suit was _____ compared to the serious-looking black coats of his companions.

3.   The car company _____ its claims about the new engine when some of the information was found to be false.

4.   Thanks to the _____ of her devoted parents, Daisy was able to skip two grades in school.

Fill in the blank with the best word from the choices below. One word will not be used.

     suspect   despicable   inoculated   advisable   evident

5.   The salesman claimed that the soap could melt away fat and wrinkles, but his promises were highly _____.

6.   Because the hurricane will probably hit land before nightfall, it is _____to evacuate the area immediately.

7.   Because Pete's mother had _____ him against the dangers of prejudice, he had friends of many different nationalities.

8.   The general's vicious personality led him to commit many _____crimes.

Fill in the blank with the best word from the choices below. One word will not be used.

     intuitive   suspect   evident   ocular   respective

9.   Dr. James' _____instrument was damaged, so he used an older model to see into his patients' eyes.

10.   The three brothers were constantly busy, as their _____jobs were in the police force, a high school classroom, and a thriving restaurant.

11.   Though Mary's anger about the loss of her boat was not _____, we knew that she was very upset.

12.   Fred's knowledge about art seemed _____rather than based on study and facts.

Exercise III. Choose the set of words that best completes the sentence.

1.   It is not _____ to wear clothing that is _____ when you are trying to blend in with the crowd.
    A. evident; suspect
    B. intuitive; despicable
    C. respective; ocular
    D. advisable; conspicuous

2.   Through the _____ of the world-famous historian, I was able to _____ and correct many of my theories about the Civil War.
    A. intuition; revise
    B. vista; inoculate
    C. tutelage; revise
    D. tutelage; inoculate

3. If Tom's cheating on the quiz becomes _____ to his teacher, she will begin to think that the results of all his previous tests are also _____.
    A. despicable; intuitive
    B. suspect; respective
    C. respective; despicable
    D. evident; suspect

4. The new educational program allows students to focus on their _____ strengths and develop a(n) _____ understanding of the material.
    A. respective; intuitive
    B. evident; suspect
    C. respective; despicable
    D. ocular; suspect

5. Because Kathleen thought that the idea of stealing was _____, she tried to _____ all of her children against it.
    A. respective; revise
    B. despicable; inoculate
    C. advisable; suspect
    D. intuitive; revise

Exercise IV. Complete the sentence by inferring information about the italicized word from its context.

1. When Krystal's dad said that she had done something *despicable,* he could have been referring to…

2. It was *evident* that Carrie hadn't studied because…

3. You rarely have a decent *vista* in the foggy city because…

Exercise V. Fill in the blank with the word from the Unit that best completes the sentence, using the root we supply as a clue. Then, answer the questions that follow the paragraphs.

The human eye is amazing. Rods, cones, nerves, and retina all combine to get an image to the brain and allow a person to "see." However, not everyone sees the same way, because disorders of the eye change visual perception.

Two of the most common eye disorders are *myopia* (nearsightedness) and *hypermetropia* (farsightedness). A myopic person is able to see things that are nearby, but finds objects beyond a certain distance blurry and hard to see. A farsighted person has difficulty focusing on things that are nearby, and sometimes on anything at all.

A person may also lack the ability to see colors. Color blindness usually involves reds, blues, and greens, so people who are affected need to develop strategies for things like clothing, stoplights, signs and warning labels.

A fourth vision problem occurs if the _____ (OCUL) nerve is damaged by injury or because of a birth defect. Today, laser technology may provide a chance to successfully reverse the damage. Laser surgery can fix the shape of the eyeball to eliminate or greatly reduce the need for prescription lenses. For all of these procedures, careful supervision of the optometrist (a person who provides glasses) or ophthalmologist (a person who prescribes eye medicines and glasses or operates on the eyes) is _____ (VIS) to ensure no harm is done to such a precious organ.

If a person is having trouble seeing, he or she may

need corrective lenses. The optometrist will advise the person about the most appropriate procedure for the condition and will administer a thorough examination to see if there is anything else _____(VID) that could be causing eye trouble. Some of the equipment looks like it came out of a science-fiction novel, but it all helps the doctor to inspect the eye thoroughly and bring anything suspicious to the patient's attention.

1. Disorders of the eye cause
   A. myopia.
   B. a person to see.
   C. different people to see different ways.
   D. visual birth defects.

2. According to the passage, a person having trouble seeing should
   A. wear glasses.
   B. undergo surgery.
   C. do nothing.
   D. consult an eye doctor.

3. When the ocular nerve is damaged, a person experiences
   A. eye problems that may be correctable by surgery.
   B. eye problems which require corrective lenses immediately.
   C. color blindness and hypermetropia.
   D. uncontrollable blinking.

4. According to the passage, what is one difference between an optometrist and an ophthalmologist?
   A. The first examines eyes, but the second cannot prescribe glasses.
   B. The first prescribes glasses, and the second examines eyes.
   C. The first can operate on eyes; the second cannot.
   D. The first cannot operate on eyes, but the second can.

Exercise VI. Drawing on your knowledge of roots and words in context, read the following selection and define the *italicized* words. If you cannot figure out the meaning of the words on your own, look them up in a dictionary. Note that *intro* means "within," and *pro* means "forward, in advance."

Of the two explorers, Francis was the more *introspective*. He liked to spend the twilight hours seated before the campfire, examining his own thoughts and feelings regarding the events of the day and the larger meaning of the whole exploration. Walter, on the other hand, tended to focus on practical matters: how far they had to travel to the next campsite, which people they would meet along the way, and how the weather would treat them. He was especially concerned about how their store of *provisions* was holding out. If they ran out of food and supplies, he knew, they would be in serious trouble.

UNIT FOURTEEN

MISS
Latin MITTERE, MISSUM, "send"

ADMISSION (ad mi´ shən) *n.*   1. Confession
                                      2. Entrance
1. Marilyns *admission* of guilt in the robbery was a surprise to those who thought she was innocent.
2. Danny was denied *admission* to the university because of his grade point average.

SUBMISSIVE (sub mi´ siv) *adj.* Tending to obey or yield
L. sub, "beneath," + missum = *sent beneath*
The court jester was ordered to be *submissive* and not to argue with the queen.

OMISSION (ō mi´ shən) *n.* The act of leaving out or neglecting
L. ob, "away," + missum = *sent away*
The only *omission* Sarah made on the application was her birth date, but that was enough for the employer to hire someone else.
                                  ant: inclusion

FER
Latin FERRE, "to carry, to bring"

DIFFERENTIATE (dif ə ren´ shē āt) *v.*   1. To set apart
                                       2. To distinguish
L. dis, "apart," + ferre = *to carry apart*
1. The only thing that *differentiated* the two species of bird was the shape of their beaks; one was slightly more rounded than the other.
2. The tornado did not *differentiate* between one neighborhood and the next; it knocked everything down.
syn: distinguish

REFERENCE (ref´ ə rens) *v.* To bring up; to mention
L. re, "back," + ferre = *to bring back*
Many history books written in 1954 do not *reference* the new polio vaccine.

TOL
Latin TOLLERE, "bring upwards, lift"

EXTOL (eks tol´) *v.* To praise; glorify
L. ex, "out of," + tollere = *to lift out of, lift up*
Most oil companies *extol* the qualities of their gasoline, but, in truth, all gas is basically the same.

TRACT
Latin TRAHERE, TRACTUM, "to drag, to draw"

DETRACT (dē trakt´) *v.* To take away
L. de, "down, away," + tractum = *to draw away*
Sally's defeat in the grammar competition didn't *detract* from Professor Nelson's opinion of her abilities in English.

EXTRACT (eks trakt´) *v.* To take out of; withdraw
L. ex, "out of," + tractum = *to draw out*
There are many ways to *extract* minerals from the ground; most involve complicated digging machinery.

GEST, GER
Latin GERERE, GESTUM, "carry, bear"

SUGGESTIBLE (sug jest´ ə bəl) *adj.* Easily influenced; susceptible
L. sub, "from below," + gestum = *able to be carried along from below*
Hypnosis works when a subject relaxes because he or she is then more open and *suggestible*.

EXAGGERATED (eks zaj´ ər āt əd) *adj.* Overstated or overdone
The ad made the *exaggerated* claim that anyone could lose two pounds a day simply by taking the vitamins.

INGEST (in jest´) *v.* To take into the body or mind
L. in, "into," + gestum = *to carry into*
To get into the world record books, Jerome had to *ingest* twelve waffles in one minute.
syn: consume

The JESTER INGESTED the goldfish.

III Traction (*from trac- tum*) *means "power to pull"; the ability of a car's tires to grip the road is an example. It also means "process of pulling"; this meaning is frequently used by doctors, who put patients with broken bones in traction—with the bones pulled in one direction— until they heal.*

III *The Latin verb* aggerere (ad, "towards," + gerere = bring towards) *means "to pile up, to gather." Something* exaggerated *is piled up very much, or very overdone.*

EXERCISES - UNIT FOURTEEN

Exercise I. Complete the sentence in a way that shows you understand the meaning of the italicized vocabulary word.

1.   The *omission* of an important piece of information in the President's speech on nuclear weapons led to…

2.   Because Darren was young and *suggestible*, he often found himself…

3.   The cartoonist gave his drawing of the king an *exaggerated* mouth because…

4.   Laura's *admission* that she had a crush on Stanley was prompted by…

5.   Walter was afraid his mood would *detract* from the joy of his sister's birthday because…

6.   Once a person has *ingested* a certain amount of the poison…

7.   Because of his color blindness, John was unable to *differentiate* between…

8.   The poet *references* many famous works in his long poem in order to…

9.   Many teachers *extol* the importance of technology in schools because…

10.   The more *submissive* dogs in the pack could be identified by…

11.   The company's attempt to *extract* copper from the riverbed was made difficult by…

Exercise II. Fill in the blank with the best word from the choices below. One word will not be used.

    submissive   exaggerated   differentiate   extract

1.   Jay, who had once been timid and _____, now stood up for himself when confronted by the bullies.

2.   A tornado does not _____ between the homes of the rich and poor; it destroys everything in its path.

3.   The _____ hairstyles of 18th century France were very different from the plain, modest styles favored in Puritan America.

Fill in the blank with the best word from the choices below. One word will not be used.

      ingest   suggestible   extract   omission   detract

4.   The files were firmly stuck in the cabinet, and we were unable to _____them.

5.   Throat cancer made it impossible for the patient to _____ solid foods.

6.   The failure of the drug was blamed on the _____ of one important ingredient.

7.   Bernice was not a very _____person; her sister, on the other hand, would agree to almost anything.

Fill in the blank with the best word from the choices below. One word will not be used.

      differentiates   extol   references   detracts   admission

8.   Roberta often _____parts of the novel *Moby-Dick* because it is one of her favorite works of literature.

9.   Although you _____the advantages of this new diet, I have no desire to go on it.

10.   The large, ugly sofa _____from the overall beauty and harmony of the room.

11.   The athlete's _____that he had actually been present at the crime scene shocked everyone.

Exercise III. Choose the set of words that best completes the sentence.

1.   When the toddler _____ some dangerous material, doctors had to _____ it from his stomach.
    A. referenced; ingest
    B. differentiated; extol
    C. ingested; extract
    D. extracted; reference

2.   Do you think that Nadine's naturally obedient and _____ personality makes her more _____ and open to the influence of others?
    A. submissive; suggestible
    B. exaggerated; submissive
    C. suggestible; exaggerated
    D. extolled; submissive

3.   Alan's _____ description of our fishing trip _____ from my memory of a lovely, simple vacation.
    A. suggestible; ingests
    B. suggestible; differentiates
    C. submissive; extracts
    D. exaggerated; detracts

4. For five dollars, we gain _____ into an exhibit that explains the characteristics which _____ one asteroid from another.
    A. admission; differentiate
    B. omission; differentiate
    C. extraction; ingest
    D. detraction; extol

5. Luke's _____ about his wild past did not stop us from _____ his virtues on a daily basis.
    A. admissions; extolling
    B. references; detracting
    C. omissions; differentiating
    D. submission; ingesting

Exercise IV. Complete the sentence by inferring information about the italicized word from its context.

1. Carrie's *admission* will probably make her parents…

2. If Bart sees no need to *extol* Zeke's athletic skills, it is probably because…

3. A crucial *omission* in the car designer's equation is probably…

Exercise V. Fill in the blank with the word from the Unit that best completes the sentence, using the root we supply as a clue. Then, answer the questions that follow the paragraphs.

Many Americans suffer from obesity, an excess of body fat that is the result of _____(GEST) more calories than are burned. Obesity is generally caused by a combination of overeating and a lack of exercise.

Unfortunately, there are a number of medical and social problems that result from it. For example, obesity greatly increases one's chances of developing diabetes and arthritis. In addition, problems like depression may be associated with obesity. Although there are a number of treatments available, most experts agree that more effort should be spent on preventing obesity than treating it.

It is, however, an extremely difficult problem to treat. Prescription drugs are available to help people control what they eat, but there are often side effects to these drugs. If a person does not find the drugs helpful, he or she can try gastric bypass surgery, a procedure in which the stomach is stapled so that it can only hold a very limited amount of food. But this option, too, comes with several risks, including hernia, gallstones, and reduction in the patient's ability to absorb vitamin B12.

Rates of obesity are increasing not only among American adults, but among American children. Overweight children are at greater risk for type 2 diabetes, asthma, high blood pressure, and skin disorders. They are also more likely than other children to develop psychological problems, since they are often teased and excluded from group activities. Because of all of these risks, many experts feel that schools should provide better nutritional education. They say that children should be taught about diet and exercise to help them _____(FER) between good and bad eating choices. If adults _____(TOL) the importance of regular exercise and encourage children to eat nutritiously, they may be able to reduce the rates of obesity among children.

1. Obesity, according to the article, is a problem for
   A. adult Americans only.
   B. children and adults in America.
   C. American children only.
   D. children in every country in the world.

2. Which of the following sentences is not true about obesity, according to the passage?
   A. Obesity can lead to health and social problems.
   B. Overweight children often have health problems when they become adults.
   C. The number of obese people in this country is declining.
   D. "Obese" means having an excess of body fat.

3. Which of the following is NOT a risk of childhood obesity?
   A. high blood pressure
   B. hernia
   C. psychological problems
   D. asthma

4. The best title for this passage would be
   A. Obesity Might Cause Health Problems.
   B. Treatment for Overweight Adults.
   C. Preventing Obesity.
   D. Overweight Children Usually Become Obese Adults.

Exercise VI. Drawing on your knowledge of roots and words in context, read the following selection and define the *italicized* words. If you cannot figure out the meaning of the words on your own, look them up in a dictionary. Note that *in* means "not" and *pro* means "forth."

George needed a lot of help with the *intractable* horse recently acquired by the stable. Even with his years of experience training stubborn and wild animals, he was at a loss as to how to manage this disobedient and unpredictable mare. He was at his wits' end, ready to *proffer* his resignation and find a new job, when Keisha appeared looking for work. As it turned out, she was a natural with difficult animals. George gladly handed her the reins and went back to the calmer horses.

UNIT FIFTEEN

FIN
Latin FINIS, "end, limit, boundary"

CONFINES (kon´ fīnz) *n.* Limits or boundaries
L. con, "together," + finis = *boundary that holds together*
As amazing as it may seem, the robber hid from the police in the cramped *confines* of the doghouse.

REFINE (rē fīn´) *v.* To make more pure or precise
L. re, "again," + finis = *to give limits to again*
The way modern companies *refine* oil to make gasoline is very different from the methods used years ago.
syn: purify, improve

FINITE (fī´ nīt) *adj.* Having an end or limit
There was only a *finite* number of seats to the show, so Maria and Elena were thrilled when their tickets arrived in the mail.

It was a FINE NIGHT, but, sadly, it was FINITE.

III *To* refine *is to make something more precise or pure. Sugar and oil can both be refined; so can a person's speech or knowledge of a difficult subject.*

CLOS, CLUD, CLOIS
Latin CLAUDERE, CLAUSUM, "to close off, to shut"

DISCLOSE (dis klōz´) *v.* To reveal; make known
L. dis, "not," + clausum = *not closed off*
Businesses are not supposed to *disclose* personal information about their employees without permission.
syn: divulge   *ant:* conceal

SECLUDE (sə klood´) *v.* To put in a private place
L. se, "apart," + claudere = *to shut apart, separate*
During the game of hide-and-seek, Jeff *secluded* himself in the basement, and he was the last one found.
syn: hide

CLOISTER (kloy´ stər) *v.* To shut away
Even though Homer was one of the richest men in the world, he *cloistered* himself away from all other people and died a lonely man.
syn: isolate

III *Claustrophobia is the fear of small or enclosed spaces. The word is a combination of the Latin* clausum *and the Greek* phobia, *meaning "fear."*

TERM
Latin TERMINUS, "end, limit"

TERMINAL (ter´ mi nəl) *adj.* Causing or forming an end
After a very long ride, we arrived at the *terminal* bus stop, and everyone got out.
syn: final, last, concluding   *ant*: first, beginning

INTERMINABLE (in ter´ min ə bəl) *adj.* Seeming never to end
L. in, "not," + terminus = *not ending*
although it seemed as if the wait for our plane to arrive was *interminable*; it actually lasted only two hours.
syn: endless, unceasing

INDETERMINATE (in dē ter´ min ət) *adj.* Not clear; not fixed
L. in, "not," + de, "from," + terminus = *not (clear) from its limits*
The scientists discovered a mummy that was so decayed that its gender was *indeterminate.*
syn: indefinite   *ant*: clear, definite

LIM
Latin LIMEN, LIMINIS, "boundary, threshold"

PRELIMINARY (prē lim´ ə ner ē) *adj.* Serving as a preparation; introductory
L. pre, "before," + liminis = *before the threshold*
Before the professional bowling tournament, Stephanie competed in the amateurs' *preliminary* tournament.
syn: first   *ant*: final

SUBLIMINAL (sub lim´ ə nəl) *adj.* Below the level of consciousness
L. sub, "beneath," + liminis = *beneath the threshold*
In that old book on differences among people, there is a *subliminal* message that one race is inferior to others, even though the book never actually states this.
syn: unconscious

Ⅲ Terminal *can apply to anything that comes to an end or stop, but it is frequently used to describe fatal illnesses or conditions. Therefore, you might board a plane at* terminal B *to see an old friend who has* terminal *cancer.*

EXERCISES - UNIT FIFTEEN

Exercise I. Complete the sentence in a way that shows you understand the meaning of the italicized vocabulary word.

1. Because our energy resources are *finite*, we will not be able to…

2. If Nicole remains *cloistered* in her dormitory, she will not…

3. In order to *refine* her performance of the ballet's central scene, Daphne…

4. The advertising campaign's *subliminal* messages made many consumers…

5. James plans to *seclude* himself in the kitchen so that he can…

6. As children, we were not allowed to go outside the *confines* of the neighborhood because…

7. When informed that his illness was *terminal*, Lance decided to…

8. *Preliminary* studies to test the side effects of the drug must be followed by…

9. Scientists said that there was an *indeterminate* number of plant species in the rain forest because…

10. The wait to see my report card seemed *interminable*, but was actually…

11. Monty would not *disclose* his reasons for leaving the examination early because…

Exercise II. Fill in the blank with the best word from the choices below. One word will not be used.

    interminable   finite   indeterminate   confines   disclosed

1. The number of possible answers to the math problem seems uncountable, but is actually _____.

2. The Office of Internal Affairs has _____ that its chief manager took bribes from several large corporations.

3. While sitting through a(n) _____ performance of the awful play, Terence found himself dozing off.

4. As long as the magician stays within the _____ of the law, he can perform any stunt he wants.

Fill in the blank with the best word from the choices below. One word will not be used.

preliminary   subliminal   indeterminate   cloister   terminal

5. Although the age of the victim is _____, we do know that she worked in an office for thirty years.

6. Eve must have some kind of _____ attraction to danger that keeps her taking risks, even against her better judgment.

7. Is the economic condition at JB Oil _____, or can it be reversed so that the company survives?

8. After the death of her twin sister, Martha wanted nothing more than to _____ herself in the house and never go out in public again.

Fill in the blank with the best word from the choices below. One word will not be used.

seclude   subliminal   refined   preliminary

9. The warden may _____ the prisoner in an isolation chamber to prevent her from doing harm to others.

10. The investigation is only _____ at this point, but has already turned up some interesting information.

11. The chemical is of a very high quality, but if it is further _____, it will be nearly perfect.

Exercise III. Choose the set of words that best completes the sentence.

1. The time left before Christopher's birthday is _____, though to him the wait seems _____.
    A. finite; interminable
    B. preliminary; subliminal
    C. refined; finite
    D. interminable; preliminary

2. Although it was cold and rainy outside, the children could not bear to _____ themselves in the _____ of the house.
    A. seclude; preliminary
    B. disclose; terminal
    C. cloister; confines
    D. seclude; terminal

3. Zeke decided that in order to _____ his knowledge of French, he would have to _____ himself in the library and do nothing but study.
    A. refine; seclude
    B. cloister; disclose
    C. seclude; disclose
    D. cloister; refine

4. The doctor decided not to _____ the truth about the patient's _____ condition until he was certain there was no cure.
    A. seclude; finite
    B. refine; interminable
    C. cloister; preliminary
    D. disclose; terminal

5. Although results from _____ tests have indicated that the drug may work, so much of the information is _____ that much more study is needed.
    A. finite; indeterminate
    B. preliminary; terminal
    C. refined; interminable
    D. preliminary; indeterminate

Exercise IV. Complete the sentence by inferring information about the italicized word from its context.

1. If Lauren *secludes* herself and ignores her friends, you may guess that...

2. If the *preliminary* results of the poll show the candidate losing the race, she may...

3. Since the walk to the bus was *interminable,* Marina most likely felt that...

Exercise V. Fill in the blank with the word from the Unit that best completes the sentence, using the root we supply as a clue. Then, answer the questions that follow the paragraphs.

It's often surprising to people that the United States prison system actually has its beginnings in religious rehabilitation. When the Quakers of Pennsylvania introduced it during America's Colonial period, they did so as part of a movement to _____ (FIN) the harsh and cruel legal codes then in place.

The members of the Religious Society of Friends, better known as Quakers, make up a plain-dressing religious sect that believes human beings can have direct communication with God without clergy, specific prayers, or sacraments. George Fox began the movement in England during the 1600's. He believed ordinary people could sit together in silent worship and feel God's presence with clarity and understanding. The Quakers' religious views, however, conflicted with beliefs held by the Church of England, and the English authorities considered Quakers to be heretics. George Fox and his followers were arrested many times.

They became dissatisfied with the criminal code, which permitted execution for most crimes and allowed torture as acceptable punishment.

One of George Fox's followers, William Penn, was granted land in America by the King of England. Penn established a Quaker colony in what is now the state of Pennsylvania, but he sought to include all people suffering religious persecution. Under his guidance, the Quaker-led legislature passed the Great Law of 1682; it declared that most crimes should be punished by hard labor in a house of correction. This law, however, did not become permanent until after the American Revolution, because the British Government was still in control of America's colonies, and it preferred the more brutal Puritan codes of corporal punishment.

In 1776, The Pennsylvania Constitution reaffirmed the Quaker code, and by 1792, the first prison was constructed on Walnut Street in Philadelphia. Each criminal was _____ (CLUD) within a cell, the theory being that isolation would compel the law-breaker to reflect upon his crime and perform "penance." This, by the way, is where we get the word *penitentiary*.

1. Why were Quakers branded as heretics?
    A. They wore different clothing.
    B. They didn't require a minister for prayer.
    C. They threatened governments.
    D. They agreed with torture.

2. What is the primary purpose of prisons, in the Quaker view?
    A. to torture criminals
    B. to give criminals a chance to think about their crimes
    C. to punish breakers of religious laws
    D. to provide education

3. What would be the best title for the article?
    A. Quakers or Prisoners
    B. Fox and the Quakers
    C. Quaker Origins of Prisons
    D. The Philosophy of Prisons

Exercise VI. Drawing on your knowledge of roots and words in context, read the following selection and define the *italicized* words. If you cannot figure out the meaning of the words on your own, look them up in a dictionary. Note that *ex* means "out."

The new airline has signed an *exclusive* contract with a major metropolitan airport in New York. From now on, all planes will begin their flights at this airport only, regardless of their destinations. The *terminus* of a flight, for example, may be in San Francisco, Texas, Hong Kong, or London; no matter where it ends, it will begin in New York.

UNIT SIXTEEN

MINISTER

Latin MINISTER, "official, minister"
MINISTRARE, MINISTRATUM, "to tend, minister, manage"

ADMINISTER   (ad min´ i stər)   *v.*   To give to; to apply
L. ad, "to," + ministrare = *to tend to*
Only rarely is a lifeguard called on to *administer* emergency treatments, but yesterday Oliver had to use mouth-to-mouth resuscitation twice.

MINISTER   (min´ i stər)   *v.*   To take care of; tend to
Being ill herself, Talia found it very difficult to *minister* to her wheelchair-bound husband.
syn: manage   *ant*: injure

The nurse was too SINISTER to MINISTER to the patient.

ARBITER, ARBITRA

Latin ARBITER, "judge"

ARBITER   (är´ bi tər)   *n.*   One who decides or determines
Even though Kelley was the *arbiter* of fashion at school, at home, all she wore was jeans and a T-shirt.
syn: judge

ARBITRATE   (är´ bi trāt)   *v.*   To judge between two sides; to referee
Janice offered to *arbitrate* the argument between two of her friends.
syn: mediate, decide, settle

ARBITRARY   (är´ bi trer ē)   *adj.*   Chosen according to whim or personal
        preference; not backed up by reason
I never choose what I'm going to wear to work for any particular reason; the decision is completely *arbitrary*.

▥ *You may have heard the word* minister *used as a noun to describe a religious official or religious duty. While this kind of* minister *certainly tends to or manages his or her flock, the verb form of the word can also be used in a non-religious sense. A nurse, for instance, might* minister *to a patient.*

MAGISTR

Latin MAGISTER, "master, teacher"

MAGISTERIAL (maj ə stēr´ ē əl) *adj.* Commanding and dignified
The mother cat led her kittens along with a *magisterial* air.
syn: regal   *ant*: unimpressive

MAGISTRATE (maj´ ə strāt) *n.* A minor civil official
To avoid being handcuffed at work, Mr. Becket turned himself in to the supervising *magistrate* in the area.

ARCH

Greek ARKHE, "ruler"
ARKHEIN, "to be first, begin"

ARCHAIC (är kā´ ik) *adj.* Dating back to a much earlier time; ancient
Many words that we use now as slang will be *archaic* in a hundred years.
syn: obsolete   *ant*: new

ANARCHY (an´ är kē) *n.* Lack of order or control
L. an, "not," + arkhe = *having no ruler*
When the king was overthrown, total *anarchy* raged throughout the country.
syn: chaos   *ant*: peace, calm

MATRIARCH (mā´ trē ärk) *n.* Female head of a family
L. mater + arkhe = *mother ruler*
In elephant society, females rule the herd; the oldest *matriarch* in the group makes all decisions for the rest of the animals.
                                   ant: patriarch

▥ *The verb* arkhein *means "to be first in time" but also "first in place or position." This is why the root gives us words having to do with power (i.e., being first in position), like* anarchy *and* matriarch, *as well as words having to do with age (or being first in time), like* archaic.

▥ *Writers, especially poets, sometimes use archaisms—words, phrases, or speech patterns from an earlier time—to make their words sound older and more serious.*

EXERCISES - UNIT SIXTEEN

Exercise I. Complete the sentence in a way that shows you understand the meaning of the italicized vocabulary word.

1.   The emergency task force *ministered* to the needs of the flood victims by...

2.   Sayeed considered himself the *arbiter* of good taste because...

3.   Pauline's *magisterial* appearance gave us all the impression that she...

4.   Dale's decision about where he would attend college seemed rather *arbitrary* because...

5.   Sandra argued that the tax laws were *archaic* and needed to be...

6.   Clarice doesn't want her dad to *arbitrate* any more of her soccer matches because...

7.   As the *matriarch* of the family, Maria was responsible for...

8.   When the surgeon *administered* treatment to revive the patient...

9.   In order to prevent total *anarchy* downtown, the city council...

10.   The couple had to go to the local *magistrate* in order to...

Exercise II. Fill in the blank with the best word from the choices below. One word will not be used.

magisterial   arbitrate   ministers   arbitrary

1.   Father Conway _____ to the poor and sick in Chestershire County.

2.   The referee is often forced to _____between furious, screaming athletes.

3.   The college president maintained a(n) _____manner both at home and on the job.

Fill in the blank with the best word from the choices below. One word will not be used.

administer   magistrates   anarchy   archaic

4.   The rebels knew that a complete overthrow of the current government would mean _____ in the country.

5.   The odd form of Russian spoken in the small, isolated village is not just old, but _____.

6.   Several _____ looked at the official document, but none of them would agree to sign it.

Fill in the blank with the best word from the choices below. One word will not be used.

arbitrates administered matriarch arbiter arbitrary

7. Camille is the _____ of the family-owned company, so any employee with a problem goes to her.

8. My history professor became the _____ of interpreting the U.S. Constitution because he had written a book on the subject.

9. Athletic trainers _____ tests to check the shortstop's reflexes and motor skills before he was hired.

10. The placement of tables in Tony's restaurant was far from _____; each was located exactly where he wanted.

Exercise III. Choose the set of words that best completes the sentence.

1. The local _____'s official job is to copy and store legal documents, but he sometimes _____ arguments between various committees in the city government.
   A. arbiter; ministers
   B. magistrate; arbitrates
   C. matriarch; administers
   D. magistrate; ministers

2. In our family, the _____ is the woman who _____ to the needs of the children when they are sick.
   A. arbiter; administers
   B. matriarch; ministers
   C. magistrate; arbitrates
   D. anarchy; administers

3. When the Mayor made the rather _____ decision to fire the entire police force, we waited for the town to break down into a state of _____.
   A. matriarch; arbiter
   B. archaic; matriarch
   C. archaic; anarchy
   D. arbitrary; anarchy

4. Desandra was the main _____ of language usage at the newspaper; her _____ attitude and tone of voice made it difficult to argue with her.
   A. archaism; magisterial
   B. anarchy; arbitrary
   C. arbiter; magisterial
   D. matriarch; arbitrary

5.   The court still _____ an oath that dates back to _____ legal practices, though many
     people have said that the oath should be updated.
     A.   administers; arbitrary
     B.   arbitrates; magisterial
     C.   ministers; arbitrary
     D.   administers; archaic

Exercise IV. Complete the sentence by inferring information about the italicized word from its context.

1.   If some of the manager's decisions seem *arbitrary,* her employees may ask for…

2.   That primitive society was ruled by a *matriarch,* so the men really…

3.   When you hear about the *magisterial* actress, you will probably expect her to play roles like…

**Exercise V. Fill in the blank with the word from the Unit that best completes the sentence, using the root
     we supply as a clue. Then, answer the questions that follow the paragraphs.**

Today, the king or queen of England is primarily a figurehead—a ruler with no real power. It is the Prime Minister who makes the important decisions. He or she leads Parliament (the British legislative body, which is much like the United States Congress) and conducts affairs of state. Royalty had real power in England for more than a thousand years, though. How did it come to pass that the monarchy lost all executive power in its own country?

Some historians have deduced that limitations on the King of England's power began in the year 1100, with the formation of the Charter of Liberties. The king, William Rufus, was harsh and unjust. He was killed by an arrow (deliberately, according to some historians). His brother Henry then seized the throne and declared, through the Charter, that justice would be the same for all. The Charter also recognized, at least in theory, that the king's power was limited; it marked the beginning of a long, uneven road towards England's present-day administration. However, many centuries passed in which various Kings enacted laws as they wished, with or without the consent of Parliament.

It was with the reign of King James I, beginning in 1601, that Parliament resolved to assert its rights and limit the king's. James I was not a wise leader and lacked the ability to compromise. His policies towards Puritans, Catholics, Scotland, and foreign affairs angered his subjects. In fact, it was because of James' injustice that the Puritans decided to leave England, going first to Holland and then settling in Massachusetts. During that time, Catholics also left Britain for Maryland. Those who stayed were subject to James' inability to properly _____ (MINISTER) his

government. He increased taxes, but failed to balance the budget, and when Parliament objected, James I dissolved it and arrested his opponents.

When James' son Charles became king in 1625, the situation became even worse, because Charles was more stubborn and insensitive to public opinion than his father had been. Anyone who opposed the new king ran the risk of being charged with treason. After three years, Parliament attempted to protect the people's rights by presenting a Petition of Rights to the king, which asked for such things as no taxes without Parliament's consent and no arrests in which the cause was not known. Charles agreed to the petition, but he quickly began to go back on his word. Then this king also dissolved Parliament and arrested some of the members, including one leader who eventually died in the Tower of London.

Charles considered himself the _____ (ARBITER) of law in England; for eleven years, he ruled the country as he pleased, without Parliament. Finally, however, a group of men met, determined to limit the power of the king. The struggle continued for almost another decade, until the country did the unthinkable and executed its own king. England suffered during the crisis, although the _____ (ARCH) some predicted never came to pass. As the centuries passed, however, the monarchs realized their powers were limited, and Parliament ruled the land. England, however, never gave up its love for the monarchy. Even today, the country honors and celebrates its royal family.

1. The best title for this essay would be
    A. A History of the English Parliament.
    B. The Misuse of Power.
    C. A Brief Survey of the Decline of England's Monarchy.
    D. The Power of Parliament.

2. The king who first took steps to limit his power was
    A. Henry I.
    B. James I.
    C. Charles I.
    D. None of the above

3. A large group of Puritans and Catholics left England during the reign of
    A. Henry I.
    B. James I.
    C. Charles I.
    D. None of the above

4. The Petition of Rights
    A. was immediately rejected by Charles.
    B. ordered that the king be executed.
    C. asked for taxes without Parliament's consent.
    D. was presented in 1628.

Exercise VI. Drawing on your knowledge of roots and words in context, read the following selection and define the *italicized* words. If you cannot figure out the meaning of the words on your own, look them up in a dictionary.

The lawyers were deadlocked for months over the meaning of a particular clause in the contract. Attorneys for the defense argued that the clause was completely modern while opposing lawyers said that it was an *archaism*, which should be eliminated from the document. When it became clear that they could not agree on this point, a judge ruled that the case was no longer *arbitrable*. It was taken out of court, and both parties went away unhappy.

UNIT SEVENTEEN

FUND, FOUND
FUNDUS, "bottom"

FUNDAMENTAL   (fun də mənt´ əl)   *adj.*   Basic and important
Belief in one God is a *fundamental* principle of many religions.

FOUNDER   (fown´ dər)   *v.*   To completely fail
The bad storm damaged one ship, and many others *foundered* in the high seas and fierce winds.

SPERS, SPARS
Latin SPERGERE, SPERSUM, "to sprinkle, to strew"

DISPERSE   (dis pûrs´)   *v.*   To cause to go in different directions; scatter
L. dis, "apart," + spersum = *sprinkled apart, scattered*
Eileen loved to see dandelions *disperse* their seeds in the wind.
                              ant: assemble

SPARSE   (spars)   *adj.*   Not plentiful; not dense
After the plague, only a *sparse* population remained in the city limits.
syn: rare   *ant:* abundant

INTERSPERSE   (in tər spers´)   *v.*   To distribute in between
L. inter, "between," + spersum = *sprinkled between*
The teacher *interspersed* a few jokes with the historical facts in his lecture.

ASPERSION   (a spûr´ zhəns)   *n.*   Negative remark; slander
L. ad, "towards," + spersum = *to sprinkle abuse on*
When I tuned in to the governor's speech. I could hardly believe the *aspersions* he was using.
syn: slur   *ant:* praise

The PERSIAN cat cast ASPERSIONS on the dry food.

⚓ *Don't get* founder *mixed up with another common verb,* flounder. Founder *means "fail"; it is what a leaky boat does in high seas, or an unprepared employee does in an important meeting. To* flounder *is "to stumble around, to thrash clumsily." A person who can't swim may* flounder *about in deep water, looking for a lifesaving device.*

MERS, MERG

Latin MERGERE, MERSUM, "to sink"

IMMERSE   (i mers´)   *v.*   To completely cover with liquid
L. in, "into," + mersum = *sink into*
We *immersed* ourselves in study because the final exam was a huge part of our grade.
syn: plung

SUBMERGE   (sub mərj´)   *v.*   To push under the surface
L. sub, "beneath," + mergere = *sink beneath*
The crew of the submarine was able to *submerge* the boat in less than ten seconds.

EMERGENT   (ē mər´ jənt)   *adj.*   Just coming into being
L. e, "out of," + mergere = *out of a sunken state*
The nation of Savanaland quickly and peacefully elected its first President; such success is rare among *emergent* nations.
syn: new   *ant:* established

FUS

Latin FUNDERE, FUSUM, "to pour out"

REFUSE   (rē´ fūs)   *n.*   Something discarded; trash
L. re, "back," + fusum = *poured back out*
The hurricane left huge amounts of *refuse* on lawns all around the town.
syn: garbage

FUSION   (fū´ zhən)   *n.*   Joining or combination
The scientists' *fusion* of two separate medical tools resulted in one that worked better than either of the originals.
syn: mixture

▥ *To* emerge *(e, "out of," + mergere = to come out of a sunken state) is to become visible from a previously covered position. Something* emergent, *in the same way, is just becoming noticeable. For instance, if doctors start to see a lot of cases of measles in town, they might say it is an* emergent *trend.*

EXERCISES - UNIT SEVENTEEN

Exercise I. Complete the sentence in a way that shows you understand the meaning of the italicized vocabulary word.

1.   The ancient castle was partially *submerged* by...

2.   In order to *disperse* the crowd of fans pushing against the stage door, the security guards...

3.   The new student was *foundering* in her math class because...

4.   After viewing the *refuse* left in the yard after the party, Nicole felt...

5.   The chef had to *immerse* the steak in olive oil in order to...

6.   When Bert cast *aspersions* on Laurel's poetry, she responded by...

7.   Because the sculpture we saw in the museum was part of an *emergent* art form...

8.   The jazz program featured many old favorites *interspersed* with...

9.   The *fusion* of old and new styles of cooking resulted in...

10. Knowledge of how a piano works is *fundamental* for a good pianist because...

11. The grass covering the pasture was so *sparse* that...

Exercise II. Fill in the blank with the best word from the choices below. One word will not be used.

aspersions   founder   interspersed   emergent   submerge

1.   Anna was afraid that if her weather predictions were inaccurate, people would heap _____ upon her.

2.   After several important employees left, the company began to _____ in the market.

3.   In order to make itself invisible to prey, a crocodile will completely _____ its body in the waters of the river.

4.   Young children need lots of games and fun activities _____ with their school lessons.

Fill in the blank with the best word from the choices below. One word will not be used.

dispersed   emergent   fundamental   refuse   sparse

5.   Once you have an understanding of the _____ principles of math, you can move on to more advanced topics.

6.   Even though the snow covering the ground was _____, the little birds could not find food.

7.   It is Hunter's job to spot _____ fashion trends so that her customers can buy the most up-to-date clothes.

8.   Matthew believed he saw gold coins in the middle of a heap of _____ and junk.

Fill in the blank with the best word from the choices below. One word will not be used.

founder   fusion   dispersed   immersed

9.   Scientists hoped to produce one large molecule from the _____ of several smaller ones.

10.   Tina _____herself in the culture of South Korea so that she could better understand the country.

11.   The rancher _____the cattle by chasing them here and there in the meadow.

Exercise III. Choose the set of words that best completes the sentence.

1.   The canoe began to _____ and was soon completely _____ in the water.
      A. immerse; interspersed
      B. disperse; immersed
      C. founder; submerged
      D. immerse; sparse

2.   Gina's _____ about Tad's artwork included the statement that "such paintings were worth no more than a pile of _____."
      A. aspersions; refuse
      B. fusions; aspersions
      C. refuse; fusions
      D. refuse; fundamentals

3.   The _____ pattern, which is just now being noticed, appears to be a(n) _____ of two previous patterns.
      A. emergent; aspersion
      B. refuse; sparse
      C. sparse; fusion
      D. emergent; fusion

4. Although farms in the area were _____, Billy was able to _____ himself in agricultural work.
   A. dispersed; founder
   B. emergent; intersperse
   C. refuse; submerge
   D. sparse; immerse

5. In the textbook, difficult ideas are _____ with more _____, basic concepts.
   A. submerged; sparse
   B. interspersed; fundamental
   C. immersed; emergent
   D. fundamental; sparse

Exercise IV. Complete the sentence by inferring information about the italicized word from its context.

1. Olive was probably *foundering* in her English class because...

2. If you *disperse* the seeds, they'll usually...

3. You can tell that the island was once *submerged* because...

Exercise V. Fill in the blank with the word from the Unit that best completes the sentence, using the root we supply as a clue. Then, answer the questions that follow the paragraphs.

Theodor Seuss Geisel, better known to his millions of fans as Dr. Seuss, wrote a large number of creative books in his career. By the time he died in 1991, he had sold over 200 million copies of his 46 books, and his *Oh, the Places You'll Go* (1990) was on the *NY Times* bestseller list. From *Horton Hears a Who!* to *How the Grinch Stole Christmas*, Dr. Seuss' books' crazy situations and unforgettable rhymes, _____ (SPERS) with colorful illustrations, captivate audiences. While the words can trip up the tongue, the stories bring smiles to the faces of kids and parents alike. In 1957, Seuss wrote the classic children's tale *The Cat in the Hat*, using only words on an average first-grader's vocabulary list. The success of the book prompted Seuss to write a series of books using an even more limited vocabulary, including *Hop on Pop, Fox in Socks,* and the timeless *Green Eggs and Ham.*

Why did Seuss use so few words? The legend is that Seuss' editor, Bennett Cerf, challenged the rhyming author to write a book using no more than fifty different words. Seuss took up the task and produced the classic children's work that many can still recite from memory several years into their adulthood.

Aside from his children's books, Seuss also worked as a political cartoonist, a documentary filmmaker, and an advertising illustrator. He also penned books under the names Theo LeSieg and Rosetta Stone.

In his long and varied career, Dr. Seuss managed to amass a following of readers that is probably unequaled in modern times. His characters are among the few in literature that live in the minds of readers long after the books are closed. His stories are imaginative, stimulating, educational, and universal. Whether you read the tales of Wockets, Whos, Grinches, bunches of Hunches, Bar-ba-loots, red fish, blue fish, or a fox in socks in English, Spanish, Italian, or any of the other 17 languages into which they have been translated, you will find yourself _____ (MERS) in the language of Seussville. In books, in films, and in the hearts of millions, Dr. Seuss' memory remains strong and ever-present, and his contribution to elementary literature _____ (FUND).

1. According to the essay, *The Cat in the Hat* is written for what grade level?
    A. 1st
    B. 2nd
    C. Kindergarten
    D. Preschool
    E. 6th

2. According to the article, Dr. Seuss worked as all of the following except
    A. illustrator.
    B. political cartoonist.
    C. documentary filmmaker.
    D. children's book author.
    E. State senator.

3. Dr. Seuss' book *Green Eggs and Ham* was written using
    A. only two-syllable words.
    B. fewer than fifty different words.
    C. fewer than forty different words.
    D. more than one hundred different words.
    E. no words with the letter O.

4. Who was Theodor Seuss Geisel?
    A. Theo LeSieg
    B. Rosetta Stone
    C. Dr. Seuss
    D. The name of the cat in *The Cat in the Hat*
    E. A, B, and C

5. The best title for this article would be
    A. The Characters of Dr. Seuss.
    B. How to Sell Millions of Children's Books.
    C. Dr. Seuss and His Creations.
    D. The Cat Who Ate Green Eggs and Ham.
    E. Horton Hopping On Pop in Seussville.

Exercise VI. Drawing on your knowledge of roots and words in context, read the following selection and define the *italicized* words. If you cannot figure out the meaning of the words on your own, look them up in a dictionary. Note that *in* means "into."

Gunther's band of soldiers was feeling tired and discouraged after their forced retreat from the mountain. To add to the difficulty, they were hopelessly lost in the deep forest, and winter was on its way. Gunther thought long and hard about how to *infuse* them with hope so that they wouldn't give up entirely. He stood where two major rivers *merged*, and spoke to his fighters about courage. He said that, just as the rivers gained strength by combining, all of the soldiers together were far stronger than one alone.

UNIT EIGHTEEN

SIST
Latin SISTERE, "stand, stop"

DESIST (dē sist´) *v.* To stop doing something; cease
L. de, "from," + sistere = *stop from, cease*
The MacNeill Shoe Company demanded in court that its main rival, Newshoes, *desist* from making sneakers with the MacNeill sole design.

ant: continue

PERSISTENT (per sis´ tənt) *adj.* Not giving up or stopping
L. per, "through," + sistere = *to stand through*
I didn't want to give the bird a cracker, but she was so *persistent* in asking that I finally gave in.
syn: unceasing

SUBSIST (sub sist´) *v.* To support life; to survive
L. sub, "beneath," + sistere = *to stand beneath, support*
A camel is able to *subsist* without water longer than nearly any other desert animal.
syn: live, exist

SED
Latin SEDERE, SEDITUM, "to sit"

PRESIDE (prē zīd´) *v.* To be in charge; govern
L. pre, "before, first," + sedere = *to sit over, rule*
Nobody wanted to *preside* over the debate in history class because everyone wanted to participate in the arguments.
syn: oversee, conduct

RESIDUAL (rē zij´ ū əl) *adj.* Left over; remaining
L. re, "back," + sidere = *to sit back, to remain behind*
The forest ranger pointed out that *residual* effects of mining were still visible more than a hundred years after the mines closed.

DISSIDENT (dis´ i dənt) *n.* One who disagrees or argues
L. dis, "apart," + sedere = *sitting apart*
The lawyers insisted that their client was not one of the *dissidents* trying to overthrow the government.
syn: rebel   *ant:* supporter

▥ Subsistence *farming is a practice which allows a farmer to grow or raise enough food to eat, but not to sell. The farmer is able to subsist on his crop, but not make a profit on it.*

▥ *The Latin* sedes, *(pronounced SEDaze) like our "county seat," meant a center of power or activity.*

▥ *To reside is to live, dwell, or exist somewhere; something resid-ual, on the other hand, is left over or left behind.*

SUBSIDIARY (sub sid´ē ər ē) *n.* One that serves or is secondary to another
L. sub, "beneath," + sedere = *sitting beneath*
Bruce worked for a *subsidiary* of the General Clothing Company in Utah, but he really wanted to be in the New York City headquarters.
syn: auxiliary

INSIDIOUS (in sid´ē əs) *adj.* Spreading harmfully and secretly
L. in, "in," + sedere = *to sit in (wait)*
The *insidious* results of the acid rain included a slow, gradual erosion of paint on cars.

ant: harmless

ASSIDUOUS (a sid´ū əs) *adj.* Determined and constant
L. ad, "toward," + sedere = *to sit towards*
James realized that unless he became a more *assiduous* note-taker in chemistry, he would never get into college.
syn: careful, attentive   *ant*: careless

SUPERSEDE (sōō pər sēd´) *v.* To make useless; to replace
L. super, "above," + sedere = *to sit above*
New, extended-length television dramas are *superseding* the old half-hour comedies.

SEDENTARY (sed´ ən ter ē) *adj.* Not very active; often in a seated position
Studies have proven that children who are *sedentary* will have more medical problems than those who exercise regularly.
syn: inactive   *ant*: lively

The SEDENTARY SENTINEL was not very successful.

> ⚶ *The Latin verb* insidere *means "to set a trap, to wait for in secret." Something* insidious *is as sneaky and dangerous as someone waiting to rob you.*

EXERCISES - UNIT EIGHTEEN

Exercise I. Complete the sentence in a way that shows you understand the meaning of the italicized vocabulary word.

1. Bobby was asked to *preside* at the meeting because...

2. The automobile *superseded* the horse and buggy as a method of transportation because...

3. Jeanne was unable to *subsist* on her original salary because...

4. Doctors were more worried about the *residual* effects of Charlene's illness than...

5. Guy knew that he would have to be *persistent* in mailing his Senator if he wanted to...

6. When the vicious king discovered a *dissident* within his political party, he...

7. The small local radio station was legally a *subsidiary* of...

8. Taylor was such an *assiduous* student that he...

9. Because Vance would not *desist* from taunting Joel...

10. When the professor discovered the *insidious* error in her students' papers, she...

11. Because she led a rather *sedentary* lifestyle, Isabel...

Exercise II. Fill in the blank with the best word from the choices below. One word will not be used.

residual   subsist   supersede   dissident   persistent

1. The food packages given to each family at the camp were small, but we managed to _____on them.

2. The new cataloging system developed by the Library Board is expected to _____ the previous system.

3. Denise hoped that her lack of interest would discourage her unwanted suitor, but he was _____ in calling and emailing her.

4. Dusty was almost completely deaf, but still had some _____ hearing from before the accident.

Fill in the blank with the best word from the choices below. One word will not be used.

     subsidiary   dissident   insidious   sedentary

5.   The _____ disease started out as a harmless rash, but could quickly turn deadly.

6.   Albert was no longer a supporter of the organization and quickly became a(n)_____.

7.   The Department of Weapons Control was not a self-ruling organization, but a(n) _____ of the Defense Ministry.

Fill in the blank with the best word from the choices below. One word will not be used.

     sedentary   insidious   presided   desist   assiduous

8.   Tan's father urged her to be more _____ in spotting and pulling out weeds from her garden.

9.   The puppy will _____ from nipping at your heels if you give her a chew toy.

10.   Alex _____ over the book club until he was replaced by a new chairman.

11.   Fran's doctor discouraged _____ behaviors such as watching television and spending hours on the computer.

Exercise III. Choose the set of words that best completes the sentence.

1.   Paula's _____ habits made it difficult for her to start an exercise plan, but she was _____ and eventually even competed in a body-building contest.
    A.   sedentary; assiduous
    B.   insidious; sedentary
    C.   subsidiary; residual
    D.   persistent; insidious

2.   When the main supply of grain disappeared, the villagers were forced to _____ on their _____ supplies.
    A.   preside; persistent
    B.   subsist; residual
    C.   supersede; insidious
    D.   preside; subsidiary

3.   The political party led by _____ and rebels may eventually _____ the administration currently in place.
    A.   subsidiaries; reside
    B.   dissidents; supersede
    C.   sedentaries; preside
    D.   dissidents; subsist

4. If a strong teacher _____ over the students, they will _____ from their bad behavior.
    A. subsists; desist
    B. presides; desist
    C. subsists; supersede
    D. desists; supersede

5. The _____ disease-causing bacteria can be carried by a person who shows no sign of illness, or it can produce symptoms that are _____ for several years.
    A. dissident; residual
    B. sedentary; dissident
    C. insidious; persistent
    D. residual; persistent

Exercise IV. Complete the sentence by inferring information about the italicized word from its context.

1. After being told to *desist* from making prank calls, Dave…

2. In dictatorships, most *dissidents* are not allowed…

3. If Reese is to *preside* over the spelling bee, she needs to…

Exercise V. Fill in the blank with the word from the Unit that best completes the sentence, using the root we supply as a clue. Then, answer the questions that follow the paragraphs.

People have engaged in some kind of athletic activity for almost as long as they have existed. An early hunter had to be in shape in order to survive, as he _____ (SIST) only on the meat of the animals he was fast enough and strong enough to kill. After a successful hunt, hunters would often travel many miles to celebrate with family; at the celebrations, there were dances that lasted many hours.

The first organized sports were related to war. During China's Western Zhou Dynasty (about three thousand years ago), there were archery competitions, cauldron-lifting contests and long-distance runs for military training. Physical fitness was also part of military preparation in the Persian Empire, Egypt, and Greece.

Sports could also provide a welcome break from battle. Ancient China had several sports for entertainment, including a competition involving throwing arrows into wine jugs, and specialized gymnastics to keep up the body's fitness. The ancient Greeks held a festival of games at the temple of Olympia (our own Olympics are named after these games). Any free male who spoke Greek was allowed to compete, and contestants traveled from all over the Greek-held lands. The games were so important that all of the Greek city-states (which often fought with one another) were bound by a truce a month before the games so that athletes could travel to the games without being harmed. And a man who competed well, or funded many athletes, in the games gained respect from his peers as well as bragging rights.

The modern-day United States also has sports for entertainment and distraction, and our military training requires grueling physical fitness training. Most American citizens, however, are neither professional athletes or soldiers. Because we spend most of our time engaging in _____ (SED) activities like computer gaming and watching television, and because we prefer cars to foot travel, our society is not as fit as some past civilizations.

1. Judging by the last paragraph, Americans would be more physically fit if they
    A. engaged in sedentary activities.
    B. had sports for entertainment.
    C. were required to be soldiers.
    D. watched professional sports.

2. The Greek city-states called a truce before the Olympics
    A. to provide a welcome break from battle.
    B. so that athletes traveling to the games would not be harmed.
    C. to mount surprise attacks on one another.
    D. to increase the athletes' feeling of harmony with one another.

3. The article mentions cauldron-lifting as
    A. one of the events in the Greek Olympics.
    B. one of the things that makes Americans less physically fit.
    C. a sport that had religious origins.
    D. an example of an ancient Chinese sport.

4. According to the first paragraph, early hunters had to
    A. be in shape.
    B. move to cities.
    C. take part in ritualized activities.
    D. socialize with family members.

Exercise VI. Drawing on your knowledge of roots and words in context, read the following selection and define the *italicized* words. If you cannot figure out the meaning of the words on your own, look them up in a dictionary. Note that *in* means "on."

The residents of Tent 5 at Camp Kenushka did not want to clean up the mess hall, but their counselor, Leslie, was *insistent*. After repeated stern orders from Leslie, the Tent 5 kids trooped down to the hall and set about attacking the terrible mess left after the food fight the night before. Part of this disgusting job included scraping a *residue* of mashed potatoes, fruit punch, and butter from the walls and floor. They did such a good job of removal that it seemed as if nothing had ever been there at all.

UNIT NINETEEN

RIV
Latin RIVUS, "stream"

RIVULET (riv´ū let)   *n.*   A small stream of water
Chicago experienced some minor flooding, but the rain gradually stopped, and only small *rivulets* of water remained in the streets.

DERIVATIVE (də riv´ ə tiv)   *adj.*   Borrowing from something else; unoriginal
L. de, "off, down from," + rivus = *to draw off another stream*
Although the author was praised for being original, most of her ideas were *derivative*.

UNRIVALED (un rī´ vəld)   *adj.*   Having no equal or competition
Many critics believe that the soprano's voice is *unrivaled* in the long history of opera singers.
syn: unequalled

UNDA
Latin UNDA, "wave"
UNDARE, UNDATUM, "to flow"

REDUNDANT (rē dun´ dənt)   *adj.*   Saying something more than once
L. re, "back," + undare = *to flow back, overflow*
When Sharon wrote in her paper about a "blazing, hot, scorching, summer July day," her teacher said the phrase was *redundant*.
syn: repetitive

ABUNDANT (ə bun´ dənt)   *adj.*   In great number; plentiful
L. ab, "from," + "undare," = *to flow from*
Spring and summer had many sunny days, so the farmers had an *abundant* harvest.
syn: plentiful

Only two burgers, but the BUNS are ABUNDANT.

ARID
Latin ARIDUS, "dry"

ARID (a´ rid)   *adj.*   Having little moisture; very dry
Ken said that if Nevada weren't so *arid*, he might consider moving there.
syn: dry   *ant*: moist

The word river, though it looks similar to rivulet, derivative *and* unrivaled, *is from a different root than these words.* Ripa, *the Latin word for* shore, *gives us our English word* river.

A rival *once literally meant "a person who shares the same stream or brook as another," i.e., a person who competes over property. It now refers to any person or thing that competes. Something* unrivaled, *therefore, has no competition.*

CLYSM
Greek KLYZEIN, "to wash away"

CATACLYSMIC   (kat ə kliz´ mək)   *adj.* Having a disastrous effect
Most scientists believe that the dinosaurs became extinct because an asteroid hit the Earth, causing *cataclysmic* fires, earthquakes, and changes in climate.
syn: catastrophic

TORR
Latin TORRERE, TOSTUS, "to burn, to scorch"

TORRID   (tôr´ əd)   *adj.*   Intensely hot or burning
The *torrid* air of the oven factory drove many people to take refuge in the freezers.

TORRENT   (tôr´ ənt)   *n.*   A heavy stream; a gush
The *torrent* of water pushed its way over the sandbags and into the main parts of the abandoned town.

DELU, DILU
Latin DILUERE, DILUTUM, "to wash away"
DILUVIUM, "flood"

DELUGE   (del´ ūj)   *n.* A flood
When William missed an easy shot that would have won the game, the fans responded with a *deluge* of booing.
ant: drought

DILUTE   (dī lōōt´)   *v.*   To water down; to weaken
If you *dilute* the acid, it will not burn anyone's skin badly.

ANTEDILUVIAN   (an ti də lōō´ vē ən)   *adj.*   Extremely old; ancient
L. ante, "before," + diluvium = *before the flood*
The oldest house on the block had such *antediluvian* plumbing that no one would buy it.

▥ A cataclysm (*cata,* "*down,*" + *klyzein*) is a flood that turns the world upside down, or a disaster so great that its effects are widely felt.

▥ What common word do you think we get from *tostus?*

▥ How could we possibly get a word meaning a "gushing stream" from a root that means "to scorch"? The answer is that *torrere* means "to burn violently, to roar like a fire," and even "to boil." A torrent *of water, as it comes rushing down toward you, seems to roar and boil in the same way.*

EXERCISES - UNIT NINETEEN

Exercise I. Complete the sentence in a way that shows you understand the meaning of the italicized vocabulary word.

1. Visitors to the mountain resort were more *abundant* this year than last because…

2. Islanders warned that if we were not careful, the *torrid* sun could…

3. When the rock star received a *deluge* of fan mail, she knew that…

4. Critics of the play say it is highly *derivative* because it…

5. Whitney complained that all her teachers were *antediluvian* and should…

6. The governor feared that the closing of the factory would have *cataclysmic* results because…

7. When local residents saw a *rivulet* of lava descending from the volcano, they…

8. Some chefs prefer to *dilute* the spicy soup because…

9. Herman's volleyball skills were once *unrivaled*, but now…

10. The *arid* landscape of North Robertsburg is not suitable for…

11. Oliver's *torrent* of words surprised everyone because he normally…

12. Frank said that calling Tina "sneaky" was *redundant* because…

Exercise II. Fill in the blank with the best word from the choices below. One word will not be used.

   abundant   unrivaled   deluge   torrent   torrid

1. During her illness, Stephanie gained a(n) _____ amount of weight because of the medicine she used.

2. When we opened the chimney for the first time, a(n) _____ of soot came streaming down into the fireplace.

3. Lester expected to receive a(n) _____ of responses to his classified ad, but instead he got hardly any.

4. The amazing economic success of Rafferty Umbrella Corp is _____ in the entire umbrella industry.

Fill in the blank with the best word from the choices below. One word will not be used.

      rivulets   redundant   antediluvian   torrid   cataclysmic   abundant

5. Compared to the _____ civilization's four thousand years of art, history and literature, our own culture seems to have just been born.

6. The damming of the large river could be _____ for the plants and animals that depend on the flow of the water.

7. As the heat of the stove increased, water boiled over and ran down the side of the pot in _____.

8. The planet's _____ atmosphere made it difficult for any life forms to grow there.

Fill in the blank with the best word from the choices below. One word will not be used.

      derivative   diluted   unrivaled   redundant   arid

9. The politician _____his strongly-worded speech for his conservative audience at the church.

10. The patient was encouraged to move from the humid jungle environment to a more _____ desert climate.

11. The speechwriter tried to think of ways to repeat the important message without being _____.

12. None of the skater's moves are _____; she invented her entire routine from scratch.

Exercise III. Choose the set of words that best completes the sentence.

1. Though water had once been _____ in Clark City, the whole area was now an _____ wasteland.
   A. abundant; arid
   B. redundant; derivative
   C. unrivaled; arid
   D. torrid; cataclysmic

2. After the _____ of water had gushed through the canyon, _____ crisscrossed the area for days.
   A. cataclysm; rivulets
   B. redundancy; torrents
   C. rivulet; cataclysms
   D. torrent; rivulets

3.   Felicia's first efforts at writing were both _____ and _____, but her later essays were brief, sharp and original.
      A.   redundant; derivative
      B.   cataclysmic; torrid
      C.   arid; redundant
      D.   abundant; unrivaled

4.   The _____ cave system contains ancient artworks _____ by any other series of cave-paintings.
      A.   rivulet; cataclysmic
      B.   redundant; torrid
      C.   antediluvian; unrivaled
      D.   derivative; arid

5.   Major climate changes, including a poisonous and _____ atmosphere, had _____ effects on all the life on the distant planet.
      A.   redundant; torrid
      B.   unrivaled; abundant
      C.   torrid; cataclysmic
      D.   abundant; derivative

Exercise IV. Complete the sentence by inferring information about the italicized word from its context.

1.   Because it was so *arid* last year, farmers had to…

2.   You wouldn't want to move to a city that had *cataclysmic* natural events because…

3.   Because water and sunshine are *abundant*, you can expect the garden to…

Exercise V. Fill in the blank with the word from the Unit that best completes the sentence, using the root we supply as a clue. Then, answer the questions that follow the paragraphs.

It is the middle of the night. A man lies sleeping in his bed. Suddenly, there is a loud pounding at his door, followed by the sound of people yelling. Then, the door crashes to the floor. The man sits up in his bed to see that police officers surround him. One of them grabs him by the arm, pulls him out of bed, and drags him from the house. His family runs after the man, but they are pushed back by the police. The man may not know why he is being taken away, but one thing is certain: he will never see his family again.

It is hard to imagine that such instances are _____ (UNDA), but they do happen to thousands of people each year. Every year, in countries all over the world, people are dragged from their homes or grabbed off the street by police or government agents. Their crime is daring to speak out against their government. People are jailed, beaten, and sometimes even killed, just for their opinions. This kind of treatment may be legal in some countries, but it is certainly not fair, and it must be stopped.

Citizens of the United States are used to being treated fairly. Americans have the right to speak out against their government. This right is promised by the First Amendment of the United States Constitution. Americans also think that all people should have the right to voice their opinions without fearing for their lives. In fact, in America, people are arrested if they physically attack others for their beliefs. Unfortunately, however, that thought is not universal. Even so, people everywhere should be guaranteed certain rights as human beings. These rights should include the ability to voice their opinions, the right to a fair trial if they should be arrested, and the right not to be tortured if they are punished for a crime. This has nothing to do with the United States or any other country in particular. It is simply respecting the fact that we are all human beings.

Everyone could join a human rights organization, like Amnesty International, that works to stop the needless torture and imprisonment of people around the world. If our government is _____ (DELU) with telephone calls, letters and email demanding an end to human-rights abuses, it will have no choice but to act. Everyone should become involved in the worldwide movement to save people from fear of torture or death at the hands of their own governments. To do anything less would be an insult to the human race.

1.   After reading this passage, we can assume that the author
     A. thinks that prisoners should be punished for their crimes.
     B. thinks that the government of a country has a right to do whatever it wants to do.
     C. thinks that all people, regardless of where they live, have the right to be treated fairly by their government.
     D. thinks that there is nothing that can be done to save people from being tortured by their government.

2.   According to the essay, the First Amendment of the Constitution is most important because
     A. it guarantees that no one in the United States will be punished for giving an opinion.
     B. the United States is governed by laws.
     C. the United States is the only country that recognizes this right.
     D. no one should say anything bad about his government leaders.

3.   According to this passage,
     A. no one should ever be arrested for a crime.
     B. if someone is arrested, torture should not be used as punishment.
     C. anyone who is arrested is innocent until proven guilty.
     D. no one should ever be punished.

4.   According to this passage, a person can help stop the unfair punishment of people around the world by
     A. joining an organization to stop the violence.
     B. organizing a rally.
     C. becoming involved in saving people.
     D. contacting local radio and television stations.

Exercise VI. Drawing on your knowledge of roots and words in context, read the following selection and define the *italicized* words. If you cannot figure out the meaning of the words on your own, look them up in a dictionary. Note that *in* means "in."

When the host of a local radio show used a word that was unfamiliar to a majority of his audience, the station was *inundated* with calls about the origin and meaning of the term. So many people phoned in that the station switchboard threatened to short-circuit, and the host decided to devote a special show solely to the *derivation* of the word. It came from an ancient Cherokee word, he explained, for the river that ran outside of the town.

UNIT TWENTY

DEIGN, DAIN, DIGN
Latin DIGNUS, "worthy"

DEIGN   (dān)   *v.*   To lower oneself to do something; condescend
Carol, the only snob among my friends, wouldn't *deign* to speak to someone who lived in the poorer section of town.

DISDAIN   (dis dān´)   *n.*   Scorn
L. dis, "apart, away from," + dignus = *away from worth*
Because Susan's dog had been spoiled, it now approached regular dog food with *disdain*.

ant: respect

INDIGNANT   (in dig´ nənt)   *adj.*   Angry at something thought to be wrong
     or unfair
L. in, "not," + dignus = *(looking at as) unworthy*
Marie became *indignant* when the store refused to honor her coupon.
syn: angry   *ant*: grateful

PREC
Latin PRETIUM, "price, worth"

APPRECIATIVE   (a prē´ shə tiv)   *adj.*   Expressing or feeling thankfulness
L. ad, "towards," + pretium = *towards a price*
Barry was very *appreciative* towards the people who gave him money for his birthday rather than clothes.
syn: thankful

DEPRECIATE   (də prē´ shē āt)   *v.*   To lose value or worth
L. de, "down," + pretium = *to go down in price*
Few items *depreciate* faster than a brand-new car; as soon as it is purchased, its value drops 35 percent.
syn: lessen, cheapen   *ant*: increase

▥ Appreciative *comes to us from the French* appriser, *which also gives us the word* appraise. *To appraise is to judge something for both positive and negative qualities.* Appreciative, *however, is often used to mean grateful.*

Jane was DEPRESSED when the stock started to DEPRECIATE.

CENS

Latin CENSERE, CENSUM, "to judge the worth of, evaluate"

CENSURE (sen´ shər) *v.*   To criticize; to blame
The United Nations voted to *censure* any country that didn't pay its dues.
syn: condemn   *ant*: compliment

CENSOR (sen´ sər) *v.*   To remove offensive material from
The school board once tried to *censor* many books but now allows almost everything in school libraries.
syn: restrict

MENS

Latin METIRI, MENSUM, "to measure"

IMMENSE (i mens´) *adj.*   Huge; enormous
L. in, "not," + mensum = *not able to be measured*
An *immense* mountain rises above the plain, dwarfing everything around it.
syn: gigantic   *ant*: tiny

DIMENSION (di men´ shən)   *n.*   A side or level of something
L. dis, "apart," + mensum = *measured apart*
When Gerald was angry, his friends saw a different *dimension* of his personality.
syn: part, aspect

COMMENSURATE (kə men´ sər it) *adj.* Equal; corresponding
L. con, "with," + mensum = *measured with*
The amount of money spent on cancer research certainly isn't *commensurate* with
the huge number of human lives taken by the disease each year.

▥ *Be careful not to mix
these two words up.
Though they come from
the same root,* censor
*means "to remove
material thought to be
offensive or harmful,"
while* censure *means
"to blame, especially in
a formal, legal situa-
tion."*

EXERCISES - UNIT TWENTY

Exercise I. Complete the sentence in a way that shows you understand the meaning of the italicized vocabulary word.

1.   The artist's paintings have *depreciated* in value over the past ten years because…

2.   The judge strongly *censured* the actions of the City Council because…

3.   Randy's personality seems to have many *dimensions* because…

4.   The pro basketball player looked with *disdain* upon my efforts to slam-dunk because…

5.   The waitress grew *indignant* when the head chef suggested that she…

6.   The audience showed that it was *appreciative* of the singer's efforts by…

7.   An official *censored* all letters from the prisoners of war so that…

8.   When the swimmer saw the *immense* body of water, he decided to…

9.   Ben would not *deign* to go to the party with Raymond because…

10.   After many years working at a low wage, Max asked for a salary *commensurate* with…

Exercise II. Fill in the blank with the best word from the choices below. One word will not be used.

deigns   appreciative   immense   commensurate   censored

1.   The _____ muscles of the professional wrestler scared away many people who would otherwise have fought him.

2.   The number of miles that Jack can run is _____with his level of physical fitness.

3.   If my self-important cousin even _____to join me for dinner, I will be very surprised.

4.   Mr. Landry claimed that his newspaper article had been _____by the government because it contained sensitive information.

Fill in the blank with the best word from the choices below. One word will not be used.

immense   disdain   depreciated   censure

5.   The worth of the silver plate has _____, rather than increased, with time.

6.   Quentin would never _____ his friend Max in public, even if he strongly disapproved of Max's actions.

7.   Although Georgia used to admire Jonathan, she now feels nothing but _____ for him.

Fill in the blank with the best word from the choices below. One word will not be used.

censor   dimension   indignant   appreciative

8.   The _____ customer refused to pay for the damaged package and said he would never shop at the store again.

9.   We must examine every _____of the problem before we can truly understand it.

10.   Leigh told us several times how _____ she was that we agreed to baby-sit at the last minute.

Exercise III. Choose the set of words that best completes the sentence.

1.   Barney did not seem _____ of our effort to get him out of jail; in fact, he did not even _____ to speak to us.
      A.   indignant; censor
      B.   appreciative; deign
      C.   immense; depreciate
      D.   commensurate; disdain

2.   A(n) _____ amount of work was required to fix up the house, which had _____ in value as it had fallen apart.
      A.   appreciative; indignant
      B.   indignant; immense
      C.   appreciative; commensurate
      D.   immense; depreciated

3.   An attempt by the newspaper to _____ the popular columnist for anti-government writings prompted several readers to write _____ letters.
      A.   censure; immense
      B.   censor; indignant
      C.   depreciate; commensurate
      D.   immense; appreciative

4.   The committee decided to _____ Judy in a way that was _____ with her minor offense.
       A. censure; commensurate
       B. deign; immense
       C. disdain; indignant
       D. censor; appreciative

5.   Frederica expressed nothing but _____ for the art form, which she said lacked any _____ and had nothing to keep the viewer's interest.
       A. depreciation; disdain
       B. disdain; dimension
       C. indigence; immensity
       D. appreciation; deign

Exercise IV. Complete the sentence by inferring information about the italicized word from its context.

1.   If the doctor is formally *censured,* he will probably feel…

2.   If the dinosaur skeleton is *immense,* the museum may…

3.   After Pete became *indignant* at the restaurant, we could assume that…

Exercise V. Fill in the blank with the word from the Unit that best completes the sentence, using the root we supply as a clue. Then, answer the questions that follow the paragraphs.

Diamonds, valued as precious stones around the world, are the hardest natural mineral known to man. They are formed from hot, carbon-rich fluids, and certain conditions must be satisfied in order for the fluids to transform. If a(n) _____ (MENS) amount of heat and pressure is present, over the course of about two to three billion years, diamonds will develop. These conditions exist only underground; experts believe diamonds form 90 or more miles deep within the Earth. Volcanic rocks carry diamonds close to the Earth's surface, where the remarkable stones then become available to humans. However, mining for diamonds is a difficult task; approximately 250 tons of ore must be mined to produce a one-carat gem-quality diamond.

Diamond mining originated in India about 4,000 years ago. Indians discovered and collected the first riverbed or "alluvial" diamonds. The earliest known reference to diamonds is in a Sanskrit manuscript from India, dated about 320-296 B.C. The country was the only known source of diamonds to Europeans until the 18th century and dominated the industry in the West until that time. In 1726, competition arose for India when diamonds were discovered in Brazil, and soon after in Borneo, creating the first worldwide diamond rushes. Still, only royalty and the wealthy had access to the revered gemstones.

Massive diamond deposits were discovered in the bed of the Orange River in South Africa in 1866, and a rush to the shores ensued. The worldwide production of diamonds from mining exploded that year, and changed the stone from a rare gem to one potentially available to anyone who could afford it. As diamond prices _____ (PREC), there was an increase in the number of potential customers, leading to the rise in popularity of diamonds as symbols of life and appreciation. South Africa soon became the largest producer of diamonds in the world, and a company called De Beers Consolidated Mines Ltd., controlled the majority of the supply of diamonds found there. Substantial diamond deposits were later found in other parts of Africa, such as Botswana, the Republic of Congo, Tanzania, Ghana, and Sierra Leone.

Currently diamonds are mined on every continent except for Europe and Antarctica. In 1979 the richest diamond deposit in the world was discovered in Western Australia, near Lake Argyle, and quickly became the area's greatest asset. Nearly one third of the diamonds produced each year now come from this region. Other dominators of the diamond production are Botswana and Russia; however, about 20 other countries also mine for the mineral. Over the last 200 years, diamond mining has become the diverse and competitive field it is today.

1.   What is the main idea of this passage?
     A.   Due to new mines, the availability of diamonds has expanded.
     B.   Diamonds were first mined in India.
     C.   Diamonds are taken from the earth.
     D.   Before diamonds were widely available, only the royalty owned them.

2.   Where did the discovery of diamonds create the first widespread diamond rush?
     A.   Orange River
     B.   Brazil and Borneo
     C.   India
     D.   Tanzania

3.   What can you infer is the result of more diamonds becoming available to the world?
     A.   Diamonds now cost more and are more valuable.
     B.   Diamonds are now used as tools.
     C.   Diamonds are smaller than earlier times.
     D.   Diamonds cost less and are more common.

4.   The majority of the world's diamonds are found in what country?
     A.   South Africa
     B.   Brazil
     C.   Europe
     D.   Tanzania

Exercise VI. Drawing on your knowledge of roots and words in context, read the following selection and define the *italicized* words. If you cannot figure out the meaning of the words on your own, look them up in a dictionary.

Amanda adopted a *censorious* attitude towards her coworkers, criticizing them constantly for even very minor mistakes. She responded to the questions they asked by rolling her eyes, making a sarcastic remark, or laughing. Soon, she was at the point where she would not even *dignify* the questions with a response; she simply pretended she hadn't heard and walked out of the room. Because she treated everyone around her as if they were not worth her time, she became an extremely unpopular employee.

VOCABULARY WORD LIST FOR BOOKS IN THIS SERIES

Book I
abbreviate
abduct
absolute
accessible
accompaniment
adjacent
aerate
aerial
affection
affirmative
agenda
airy
alleviate
ambition
analogy
apologetic
appendix
application
apprehend
ascertain
asocial
aspire
associate
assumption
attentive
attractive
ballistic
biographical
brevity
brutality
brute
capacity
capitalize
captivate
celebrant
celebratory
celebrity
certainty
certify
circumstance
coagulate
companionship
complex
composition
comprehend
compute
concerted
condense
conduct
confidante
confident
confirm
conscience
conservative
constant
constrict
consume
contract
convection
convict
cooperate
course
creed
currency
decapitate
deficient
deflate
defunct

deliverance
delude
denounce
density
deposit
descriptive
diagram
discount
discredit
disintegrate
dismantle
dispense
distract
domestic
domicile
dominate
dominion
duplicate
effortless
elevate
elongate
emaciated
emancipate
encompass
evaluate
evict
exhilarating
expire
fabled
fabulous
facsimile
fortify
fortitude
frugal
fruitful
gradual
grave
gravity
hilarity
host
hostile
hyperventilate
ideal
idealistic
idealize
illogical
illusion
impermanent
impress
incredible
infirm
inflate
inoperable
integrate
integrity
intend
invalid
invaluable
jubilant
jubilee
leverage
levitate
liberal
liberate
linguistic
literal
literate
malfunction
mantled

manual
manufacture
manuscript
meager
militant
militarize
multilingual
mythical
mythology
narrate
narrative
obliterate
observant
occurrence
omnipotent
operational
opponent
oppress
oral
oration
oratory
parable
passable
petrify
possessive
potent
preservation
presumptuous
procession
produce
program
progression
projectile
prolong
pronounce
proposition
prosecute
rapidity
rapture
recipient
recount
recurrent
regal
regicide
reign
remnant
reputation
restriction
reveal
savor
savvy
scientific
sensation
sensible
sentimental
sequel
sequence
sociable
socialize
solution
spirited
stationary
status
subject
subscribe
succession
suffice
sumptuous
suspend

symbolize
textile
texture
transact
transgress
transit
unveil
validate
vehicle
ventilate
victorious

Book II
abhor
abundant
accelerated
administer
admission
advisable
agile
agitate
allege
amnesty
anarchy
annals
annual
annuity
antediluvian
anticipate
appreciative
arbiter
arbitrary
arbitrate
archaic
arid
aspersion
assiduous
astronomical
autonomous
avail
castigate
cataclysmic
celestial
censor
censure
chastened
chastise
chronic
chronology
cloister
cohabitation
commensurate
composure
conceive
condone
confines
connoisseur
consolidate
conspicuous
contemporaneous
contemporary
corroborate
deceptive
deify
deign
deity
deluge
demented
demote

depreciate
derivative
desist
despicable
deter
detract
diagnosis
differentiate
dilute
dimension
disclose
discourse
disdain
disperse
dissident
donor
durable
duration
editorial
emergent
enact
enduring
energetic
enumerate
ergonomic
evident
exaggerated
exceptional
excursion
exhibit
exhume
exponential
extol
extract
finite
formidable
forte
fortitude
founder
frequent
fugitive
fundamental
fusion
horrific
humility
hypothesis
idiom
idiosyncrasy
immense
immerse
immovable
imposition
impunity
inconstant
indeterminate
indignant
infrequent
ingest
innumerable
inoculate
insidious
instantaneous
insular
insulate
inter
intercept
interminable
intersperse
intimidate

intrepid
intuitive
inveterate
invigorate
irreverent
jurisdiction
jurisprudence
litigant
litigation
magisterial
magistrate
matriarch
mentality
minister
mnemonic
mobile
monotheism
nebulous
nemesis
nimbus
nonplussed
nontraditional
notorious
ocular
omission
pantheon
parenthetical
participant
perjure
persistent
plurality
polytheistic
preliminary
preside
prodigal
prognosis
punitive
ration
rational
reactionary
reconnaissance
redundant
reference
refine
refuge
refuse
reinstate
repository
residual
respective
revere
revise
rivulet
robust
sanctify
sanctions
sanctuary
sanctum
seclude
sedentary
single
singular
solidarity
sparse
stellar
subliminal
submerge
submissive
subpoena

subsidiary
subsist
subterfuge
subterranean
suggestible
supersede
surgical
surplus
suspect
syndicate
synthesize
tempo
terminal
terrestrial
terrorize
timorous
torrent
torrid
trepidation
tutelage
unrivaled
valiant
valor
veteran
vigorous
vista
volatile

Book III
abjure
abstain
accord
adept
affable
affiliate
affluent
agenda
alias
alienate
allegation
alleviate
alteration
altercation
alternate
amble
ambulatory
amiable
amicable
analogous
animosity
anonymous
antagonist
antagonize
antebellum
antibiotic
antonym
aptitude
aristocracy
assonance
audit
auditory
bellicose
belligerence
benefactor
benevolent
benign
bibliophile
biodegradable
bureaucrat

cadence
casualty
cede
circumspect
cognitive
cognizant
collapse
concession
confound
conjure
consecutive
cordial
corporeal
corpulent
courier
decadent
delegate
denomination
deplete
dialogue
dictum
digress
dilate
diminish
discord
disenchanted
dismal
dispel
disposition
dissemble
dissonance
divest
domineering
edict
effigy
elapse
elucidate
enamored
enjoin
enunciate
equanimity
equilibrium
equitable
exacting
execution
expatriate
expedient
figment
filial
formative
genealogy
gradualism
herbivorous
homogenized
homonym
immortalize
impart
impartial
impediment
implement
impose
improvise
inalienable
inaudible
incantation
incision
inclusive
incognito
inconclusive

inconsequential
incorporate
incur
indecisive
indict
indomitable
ineffable
inept
infantile
infuse
inhibit
iniquity
injunction
invidious
invoke
leaven
legacy
legislative
legitimize
levity
lucid
magnanimous
magnate
magnitude
malevolent
malicious
maternal
matriculate
matron
maxim
megalomaniac
megalopolis
mellifluous
metabolism
metamorphosis
metaphorical
microcosm
microscopic
miniscule
minute
misinformation
monogamy
monolithic
monologue
monopolize
morbid
moribund
mortify
nomenclature
nominal
noxious
omnivorous
partisan
paternal
patricide
patronize
pedagogue
pedant
pedestrian
perceptible
perjury
pernicious
philanthropy
philosophical
phosphorescent
photogenic
phototropic
posit
preamble

precept
precise
preclude
predominant
prefigure
privileged
proactive
progenitor
progeny
prohibit
prologue
pronouncement
propel
prospect
protagonist
providential
provocative
rapacious
rapt
recant
recede
recurrent
reform
regress
rejoinder
relapse
relative
renounce
replete
repulsion
resonant
retinue
revival
revoke
semblance
simulate
sophisticate
sophistry
sophomoric
specter
suffuse
superfluous
superlative
surreptitious
susceptible
sustain
symbiotic
synonymous
tenacious
theocracy
translucent
travesty
unanimous
uniform
unison
vested
vestment
vivacious
vivid
voracious

Book IV
aberrant
abject
abrogate
acerbic
acquisitive
acrid
acrimonious

adherent
admonition
adverse
advocate
aesthetic
anatomy
anesthetic
annotate
antipathy
apathetic
apolitical
apparition
approbation
arrogant
aspect
avarice
avid
benediction
bibulous
cautionary
cautious
circumvent
civic
civility
civilize
clamorous
colloquial
compel
complacent
comportment
compunction
conciliatory
concise
conducive
confer
confide
congress
conjecture
connotation
conscientious
constructive
construe
convene
convoluted
correspond
cosmopolitan
counsel
covenant
credence
credible
credulity
crucial
crux
culpable
culprit
cursory
declaim
decriminalize
deduce
defer
deference
definitive
deflect
degrade
dejected
demagogue
demographic
denotation
deprecate

derogatory
despondent
destitute
deviate
diaphanous
dichotomy
dictate
diffident
diffuse
diligent
dismissive
dispute
disreputable
dissolute
dissuade
docile
doctrine
doleful
dolorous
dubious
effervescent
effusive
egress
eloquent
emissary
emote
empathy
envisage
epiphany
epitome
equivocate
errant
erroneous
espouse
evince
evocative
evolve
exacerbate
excise
exclamatory
excruciating
exonerate
expel
expound
extort
facile
facsimile
factotum
fallacious
fallacy
fallible
fervent
fervor
fetid
fidelity
fractious
glut
glutton
gratuitous
gustatory
gusto
imbibe
impervious
impetuous
impetus
imprecation
impulse
impute
incisive

incoherent
incredulous
incriminate
incursion
indoctrinate
indolent
indubitable
induce
inference
infinite
infinitesimal
inflection
inflexible
infraction
infrastructure
infringe
ingrate
ingratiate
inherent
innovative
inquisitive
insipid
insoluble
intact
intemperate
interrogate
intractable
introspective
invincible
irrational
locution
malediction
malodorous
mea culpa
motif
motive
novel
novice
obviate
odoriferous
olfactory
onerous
onus
palatable
palate
pandemic
pathos
penultimate
perspicacious
persuasion
petulant
phenomenon
placebo
placid
politicize
precarious
precaution
precursor
premonition
prescient
presentiment
primacy
primal
primeval
proffer
proficient
profuse
proliferate
proponent

protracted
provincial
punctilious
pungent
purported
putrefy
putrid
rancid
rancor
rationale
rationalize
recollect
reconcile
recourse
recrimination
redolent
redoubtable
remiss
reprobate
reprove
requisition
resolute
restitution
retort
retract
retrospective
revert
sacrilege
sapient
sentient
sentiment
sentinel
stagnant
stagnate
stature
subvert
sycophant
tactile
tangible
temper
temperance
tome
tortuous
ultimate
ultimatum
unconscionable
viaduct
virile
virtue
virtuoso
visage
voluble

Book V
ablution
abominable
abomination
accede
acclivity
acquiesce
adorn
adventitious
alluvial
ambiance
annex
antecedent
appall
append
appraise

appreciable
apropos
ascertain
assertion
attrition
auspices
auspicious
bacchanal
bacchic
belabor
candid
candor
catholic
cavernous
certitude
circuitous
communal
concave
conferment
conflagration
congested
consort
consortium
consummate
contort
contravene
contrite
converge
crevasse
crevice
declivity
decorous
decorum
demerit
demonstrative
denigrate
depose
deracinate
desolate
destine
desultory
detrimental
detritus
discomfit
disconcert
disseminate
dissertation
distill
distort
diverge
divulge
ecstasy
edification
elaborate
elegiac
elegy
entity
eradicate
essence
euphoria
excavate
excommunicate
exertion
expendable
extant
exultant
feasible
festoon

fete
fission
fissure
flagrant
flamboyant
florid
flourish
fluctuate
fluent
formality
formulaic
formulate
fortuitous
fortuity
fulminate
germane
germinal
germinate
gestate
gesticulate
hiatus
hoi polloi
holistic
illustrative
illustrious
impair
impeccable
impending
implicit
importunate
importune
incandescent
incendiary
incense
incommunicado
inexplicable
inflammatory
inordinate
insinuate
instill
insufferable
interject
inundate
irradicable
jocose
jocular
laborious
lachrymal
lachrymose
languid
languish
languor
lavish
lenient
lenitive
lethargy
liaison
ligature
liturgy
livid
luster
magnum opus
malaise
malfeasance
malign
malinger
meander
meretricious

meritorious
metaphrase
modus operandi
mollify
monosyllabic
monotone
monotonous
munificent
negate
negligent
negligible
nexus
obligatory
ominous
opulent
ordain
orifice
ornate
orotund
pallid
pallor
paradigm
paraphrase
parcel
parse
parvenu
peccadillo
peccant
pejorative
periphery
phraseology
plaint
plaintive
polyglot
polymath
precedent
predestine
preferential
preordained
proclivity
propitiate
propitious
quintessential
quittance
rapport
redound
refulgent
remonstrate
remunerate
repartee
requiem
resilient
restive
riparian
rudiment
rudimentary
sedition
semantic
seminal
semiotic
sinuous
soliloquy
solipsism
somnolent
sopor
soporific
stanch
stasis

static
staunch
subjective
suborn
summation
surfeit
synergy
totalitarian
totality
transitory
trenchant
trite
truncate
undulate
verdant
verdure
vigilant
vigilante
viridity
vulgar

Book VI
abscond
abstruse
adduce
adjourn
adjudicate
adroit
adumbrate
aggregate
agrarian
alacrity
allocate
allude
amoral
anachronism
anathema
animadversion
aperture
apocryphal
apposite
apprise
artifice
artless
ascribe
aspire
assay
asset
attenuate
avocation
bucolic
capitulate
caprice
celerity
chronicle
circumlocution
circumscribe
cogent
cognate
colloquy
collusion
complicity
composite
comprise
concede
concordance
concur
confluence

conjugal
consecrate
consign
conspire
constrain
contend
context
contiguous
contingent
covert
cryptic
defray
degenerate
demise
demur
demure
derisive
devoid
diabolical
discern
discordant
discrete
discretion
discursive
distend
diurnal
dour
duplicitous
duress
dystopian
egregious
emblematic
emulate
engender
ensue
episodic
epithet
esprit
evanescent
execrable
exigent
expiate
explicate
extemporaneous
extenuating
feign
felicitous
felicity
fictive
flux
fruition
fruitless
genre
gregarious
hyperbole
icon
iconoclast
iconography
idyllic
impious
implicate
in lieu of
inanimate
incessant
incite
inconsolable
incorrigible
incurious

inert
inexplicable
infelicitous
influx
infrangible
inimitable
innate
innocuous
insatiable
insuperable
intercede
interlude
internecine
interpose
intransigent
intrusive
inveigh
irrepressible
judicious
locus
loquacious
ludicrous
magniloquent
methodical
moratorium
mores
morose
myopic
nascent
obdurate
obloquy
obsequious
obtrusive
ostensible
overt
parturient
pastoral
peregrination
perpetuate
perpetuity
pertinacious
perturb
plenary
plenipotentiary
portend
precipitate
prestige
pretext
procure
proscribe
proviso
psyche
psychosomatic
psychotic
purveyor
purview
pusillanimous
recapitulate
recondite
rectify
rectitude
refract
remit
repast
repertory
reprehensible
reprimand
reserved

resignation
resuscitate
reticent
risible
rustic
sacrosanct
salubrious
salutary
salutation
satiety
sectarian
segue
servile
signatory
sinecure
sojourn
solace
solicitous
sovereign
stricture
stringent
subdue
subjugate
subservient
subtext
succor
suffrage
suppress
surfeit
surmise
synchronous
synod
synopsis
tacit
taciturn
temporal
temporize
tenable
tendentious
tenet
tenuous
topical
traduce
transect
transfigure
transpire
turbid
turbulent
umbrage
univocal
utopian
vacuity
vacuous
vaunted
vehement
verbatim
verbiage
verbose
vocation
vociferous